# A.B. Roveen

# Ned Bear and the Dirty Whisker Curse

Great things have small beginnings.
- Sir Francis Drake

*To my wife, everything.*

*To my three endearing children, if it wasn't for you this book would have been done five years ago. I wouldn't trade a single moment of it. I hope someday you read this, and it fills the sails of your imagination.*

# Contents

# Chapter 1
# The Bear Down by the River

Dripping wet after wading in the river, Ned the grizzly bear stripped off his shirt and hung it on a nearby tree. He kept his breeches on for decency. The area, after all, wasn't entirely deserted.

He lay back in the tall grass along the bank of the Muddy River, his brown fur already starting to dry under the mild morning sun. His limbs were heavy after catching three stripers for his midday meal. He was in no hurry to cook his fish, this being his day off from the sulfur mine. Lying in the soft grass under the clear blue sky for a while longer appealed to him far more. Catching salmon had never been this hard back home. It was easy to see them in the streams, and they jumped right into his paws.

A lump dropped into his throat that made it hard to breathe. He shook his head, trying to force the thoughts of home out of his mind. He missed his home, but he could never go back. Desertion was an unforgivable crime. His family would've heard what he'd done by now, but they'd never find him. No one would look for him this far south. He hadn't regretted what he'd done, only that he hadn't said goodbye to his mother. His head pounding, tears stung his eyes at the thought of her.

*Time to think about something else. I wonder what I'll catch in the bay tonight. Maybe I'll borrow a barge so I don't have to fish off the shore.*

With the sharp tips of his claws, he snagged his leather pack to make a note in his journal about fishing in the river. However, before he could open it, the sun won, and he surrendered to his exhaustion. The sunshine warmed his fur while the birds sang him a sweet lullaby. He closed his heavy eyelids and drifted off to sleep.

Ned jerked awake, gasping for air. The familiar sounds of clashing steel and ferocious roars made his heart lurch into his throat.

*They found me. Where are my axes?*

He swatted at the grass, momentarily forgetting he had thrown his axes into the ocean months ago. He whipped his head around to wake himself up faster, his tongue slapping his whiskers. He took a deep breath to regain focus and tilted his head to listen.

*Those aren't bears. Otters and jaguars?*

The battle called to him like all the others before. He needed to know what was going on.

Ned tucked his dagger into his belt. He trotted up the slope of the riverbank on all fours to find three otters surrounded by the Wexlin city guard. A tall, skinny otter held a short, single-edged saber in each paw. The city guard, made up of six jaguars in unkempt green armor, laughed and taunted the otters with their spears. The skinny otter parried one spear away and spun back around, looking for the next attack. A stocky otter with a blue vest and red breeches pointed his pistols at the jaguars. His eyes wide, he seemed uncertain whether to fire at them.

The pair protected a third otter with a flat chin. His hands trembled, his sword and pistol posing little threat to the guards.

"Hello," Ned said.

The city guard froze and stared at him. The otters took the opportunity to flee.

Another otter in polished green armor atop a saddled young elk rode up from behind the jaguars. Ned hadn't seen him at first, but he was hardly worried about an otter, even if he was mounted. He snorted. Especially with his mount having mere stubs for antlers.

"You've interfered with the duties of the Wexlin city guard." The otter halted his mount in front of Ned. "This is a crime punishable by a fine and military service to the governor of Wexlin. What business do you have here?"

"I wasn't aware saying hello was a crime in Wexlin." Ned playfully scratched at the elk's chin.

"You will address me as 'my lord.' Lord Colin Gallant. It will serve you well to remember it."

Ned yawned.

Gallant clenched his jaw. "Help us catch those thieves you let escape, and your crime is forgiven."

The jaguars crept forward behind their square shields, their spears pointed at Ned.

"Otter, I'm not joining your army. Your ranks are fine without me." Ned nodded at the jaguars.

Gallant frowned. "Six gold coins every new moon, officer daily wages, endless rations, and custom armor and arms."

*That's more than I made as a soldier for an entire summer.* "Your offer is more than generous. But I must still refuse, *my lord.*"

Gallant looked down his nose at Ned. "Why do you refuse me? Refuse to serve the governor and the city you dwell in?" He tilted his head. "Are you a coward? A bear who refuses to fight for money? It's absurd. I've been watching you since you arrived here. Do you really want to live off scraps, digging holes in that stinky mine?"

"Dirt is easier to wash out of my fur than blood."

"Fine. If I can't recruit you with reason, it will be by force."

Gallant spun his mount out and retreated behind the jaguar shield wall.

"You don't have enough spears." Ned stood on his hind legs, casting a shadow over the approaching jaguars.

He extended his claws and gave them a fierce growl as a final warning. These were hardly professional soldiers. Just a bunch of cats playing dress-up and collecting coin. Ned roared. All of his aggressors froze except one. Was he brave or stupid?

The jaguar lunged forward and thrust his spear weakly. Ned grabbed the spear by the shaft, yanked the jaguar toward him, and smacked him with the back of his paw. The jaguar and his helmet flew backward. Ned smiled. A basic defensive maneuver. He'd learned to disarm a single spear right after he'd learned to walk. He snapped the spear in half and tossed it at the other jaguars' feet. Yowling, they lifted their fallen comrade and retreated back to the city.

"This isn't over, bear. I'll see you in chains or a uniform by spring." Gallant chased after the jaguars.

Ned scoffed at him. *Well, I was never going to get to stay here forever.*

He rushed back to his campsite to gather his things in case Lord Gallant brought the army after him. That otter was never going to leave him alone. Every lord wanted a bear in their ranks, so Ned expected offers like this. He had received similar ones on his journey south to Wexlin, but he didn't abandon his family to become a sellsword. He could've stayed home if he wanted a fight. He only came to Wexlin to learn more about the great otter explorer Ulrich Leon Labarre.

"Oy! You there, bear?"

Ned glanced up the riverbank. The three otters who had fought the jaguars pointed down at him. The sun bounced off their swords and pistols, causing Ned to squint.

The skinny one in the middle held up his paw to silence the

others. "Bear, I just wanted to thank you for your aid. We were hoping we could repay you for—"

"Helping you escape?" Ned growled. "I suggest you and your friends move along before they come back."

"Naw, don't worry about them, mate," said the stocky otter. "They're likely very busy right now."

Ned raised an eyebrow.

"Word around town is the grain store is being robbed at midday," the otter with the flat chin said. "Trust us. We're safe here for now."

"I don't trust you." Ned smirked. "I didn't mean to help you escape, and now, thanks to you three, I've got that Lord Gallant after me."

Flat Chin walked down the riverbank, too close for Ned's comfort. Ned whipped around and stood up on two legs. His shadow stretched across the tall grass, putting the now timidly approaching otter in complete darkness. Ned released a low growl. Bears often walked around on all fours to make other creatures more comfortable, but this armed otter's approach made him forgo courtesy.

The otter removed his tricorn hat and bowed his head. "My name is Tino." He unbuckled his belt, and his sword fell onto the grass. "My intentions are honest. We just want to repay you with a small feast."

Ned snarled. "You wish to repay me by eating my rations?"

"No. No. That's not our intention." Tino nervously pulled at a whisker. "You see, I'm somewhat of a cook myself."

The stocky otter with the blue vest and red breeches snorted. "No one has ever accused him of being a cook!"

Tino shot him a withering look. "Quiet, Norbert. Bear, please hear me out before you decide to eat me."

Ned lowered himself onto all fours. His paws pounded the grass with as loud a thud as he could make. He lowered his head and eyed Tino. He glanced up the bank toward Norbert and the other one to make sure they hadn't pulled their weapons. Shaking, Tino avoided eye contact with Ned.

Ned flared his nostrils. "State your intent, otter."

"My mate up there, Pierre..." Tino said.

Ned peered at the scrawny otter. Pierre slowly waved.

Ned focused on Tino. "What about him?"

"Well, he's a great fisher. One of the best. We used to fish this river all the time when we were pups. You see, he'll catch some fish. We won't even eat your rations. And I'll cook it for us. We'll do all the work. A small token of our tremendous gratitude."

Ned was, much to his surprise, intrigued. *What an odd request.* A heavy weight settled in his chest. He had eaten every one of his meals alone since coming to Wexlin six months ago. Tears stung his eyes. He had been alone for eleven months since leaving home.

"My name is Ned," he grumbled, then adopted a friendlier tone. "Pierre, Norbert, Tino..." He made eye contact with each of them. "I would like to have a meal with all of you."

All three otters blew out breaths, then cheered.

"However..."

The otters froze.

"I'll be doing the cooking. I've been looking forward to doing so all morning."

Pierre removed his weapons, boots, and shirt, then jumped into the Muddy River. Norbert came down the bank and sat next to Tino.

"Oy, Ned, shouldn't you be sleeping?" Tino asked. "It is wintertime and all. Isn't that what you bears do?"

"Most do." Ned rummaged through his pack for his cooking journal. "It's sort of an old bear tradition that dates back to before we could read and write. Helped us save rations. But here there are no other bears and plenty of fish."

"Yeah, and there ain't no winter snow here either." Norbert hovered over Ned's pack. "What's in your bag?" He picked it up and pulled out a book.

Ned's fur stood on end, and he tensed. "Don't go through my bag."

Wide-eyed, Norbert froze and dropped the pack but still clutched the book. He held it up and touched the seal of the round bird on the center. "You know Labarre?"

"I do. I've read his books. Please be careful with that. I'm borrowing it from a friend."

Tino peeked over Norbert's shoulder. "How'd a bear stumble upon a book written by an otter?"

"I read them as a cub in bear school."

They stared at Ned. "Bear school?" they said in unison.

"Yeah. It's a place where all young bears go to learn to be bears. I found a copy of Labarre's first book, *The Land of Only Man*. It had been scribbled in and was missing a few pages, but I still read it several times. Some old bear must've left it behind, so I did the same when I left."

He didn't tell them he'd read it at least a hundred times and dreamed about being an explorer just like Ulrich Labarre.

"Look," Norbert said to Tino. "He's reading the treasure one."

Tino's gaze darted to Norbert, and he elbowed him in the ribs.

"What treasure?" Ned asked.

"You haven't finished the book, so I won't spoil it for you. What brings a bear all the way down the Great Divide here to Wexlin? The city's gossip claims you're the first bear to ever visit these lands."

Ned hardly knew these otters and didn't see a reason to tell them the truth—that he had marched north with all the other bears from his town and simply had lost the will to go to war. They never told him what the war was about. Just some rich bear mad at another rich bear. He had never met the bear he was supposed to die for and didn't see the point in fighting for him. On the next night's march, Ned fell behind the rest of the bears, tossed his axes and armor into the ocean, and headed east. At first, he hadn't known where to go until he realized there was only one place he wanted to go. He would start his new life in Wexlin where Labarre had started his.

"Just wanted to avoid hibernating this year and to learn a new way to cook fish."

Tino tilted his head and studied him for a moment. If he knew Ned was lying, he didn't say so. "All right then. I'll see if Pierre has any fish to fillet. Norbert will tend to the fire."

Ned took a sip from his water sack and swished it around. He pulled his pack closer and watched Norbert from the corner of his eye. He didn't trust these otters, but he was excited by the prospect of having some companionship, even if it was just for one meal.

# Chapter 2
# The Otters Three

Two ravens squawking over fish heads and guts woke Ned. He and the otters had eaten, talked, and fallen asleep for an afternoon nap. The fire had gone out, and there were still a few leftover steaks warm on the grill. A large catfish, six stripers, and an assortment of bass Pierre had caught were more than enough to feed the four of them. Ned couldn't help but chuckle at the sleeping otters. He thought he was going to wake up alone without any of his things.

He collected whatever meat he could save and placed it in his sack along with his cooking supplies. By then, the otters had awoken. Pierre tended to the fish he caught and strung them all up through the gills and onto a branch.

Tino walked in circles. He finally settled on rigging some rope to carry a large catfish without cutting it. Norbert sat up and watched them. He rubbed the black fur on his chin and upper lip that clashed with the auburn of the rest of his body. When he found there was nothing to do, he stretched and lay back down in the tall grass.

"Well, Ned, I hope this is only farewell for now." Tino extended his dark-brown paw.

"Anytime you three are in port, I'd welcome the company."

Ned went to slide his paw pad over Tino's. Instead, Tino grabbed Ned's pointer claw with his tiny paw and shook.

"Tonight. Cook, drink, and eat with us." Pierre shook Ned's finger as well.

Tino grabbed Pierre's shoulder. "Tonight I have to cook at the officers' meeting."

Norbert sat back up. "It's going to be about Labarre. Ned should cook with you. Or better yet, instead of you."

Tino threw a small rock and hit Norbert in the leg. He fell like he had been shot.

"Officers? I'm not interested in a recruitment dinner." Although Ned was curious what it had to do with Labarre.

"No, it's not like that." Norbert stood. "Just a routine meeting that Tino is supposed to cook at. To be honest, I just can't stomach his slop anymore."

Tino put his paws on his hips. "You're lucky I don't poison every last one of you."

"It would be a mercy kill to do so." Norbert snorted. "Please, Ned. We'll pay you for helping Tino. You'd be doing us a favor."

Ned wasn't sure if Norbert's intentions were sincere, but his stomach fluttered at the prospect of cooking for and meeting more new creatures. "I could cook again tonight. But I'm not joining your gang or ranks."

"Fair enough." Norbert patted Ned's leg. "See you tonight."

"Well, I suppose I could use some help," Tino said.

"And everyone's bellies will be grateful for it." Pierre hauled the fish onto his shoulders.

"Can I pay you for those fish?" Ned searched in his pack for coin.

Pierre chuckled and dropped the bundle. "They're yours, Ned.

I don't wish to haggle with a bear, nor do I wish to be around one who is hungry. Take all the fish as another token of our gratitude."

Ned frowned. "I can pay for them."

"No, take the fish," Pierre said. "If you want to pay me, just be at the Sleeping Crawfish at sunset to help Tino."

They exchanged goodbyes, and the otters merrily walked toward the city.

Ned grabbed his pack, the rest of his supplies, and the bundle of fish. He lifted the large catfish by the tail and balanced it on his shoulder, being careful not to get its scales on his pack, then headed into town.

The catfish had stopped dripping down Ned's legs by the time the dirt road turned into a cobbled street. Wexlin was known as "Crescent City" for the way it curved around the ocean until it met the bay. There was only enough room on the small strip of land for the eastern road—a road Ned had not traveled but had heard it led into red fox lands. It was a small kingdom, but it was not one the otters ever provoked.

For the first two months Ned had lived in Wexlin, he had thought they were calling it the "Cathedral City." This had made sense because of the ridiculous cathedral that dominated the center of the city. The four bell towers echoed over the city every hour, day and night. During the day, the cathedral cast the smaller surrounding buildings and the horde of starving creatures camped in its courtyard in complete darkness.

Some of the otter, puma, beaver, and red fox younglings of the horde spotted Ned and started following him. He smiled and winked at them. This had become a playful tradition. He often let the younglings ride on his back whenever he was in town and fed them scraps of food. This was why he wanted Pierre's fish.

Ned traveled down Harbor Road. The refreshing salty air filled his nose, taking his mind away from the smell of the city's filth. Gulls, pelicans, and a few blackbirds perched on the rock wall and neighboring lampposts, all of them very interested in Ned's fish. Several birds pursued him, some hopping along the wall beside him, others flying from lamppost to lamppost. With the birds and younglings following him, Ned felt like he was leading a parade through the harbor.

From this road, he had a nice vantage of the tall ships anchored at sea. Coming from the mountains of the west, he had never seen large wooden ships. Most of the vessels he'd encountered were canoes that could be carried over land.

These ships were like fortresses on the water, each with flags flown from the center masts. How could something so big and heavy float? He was fascinated by all the different types of ships anchored in the harbor. He gulped, terrified of being on such a ship surrounded by nothing but empty ocean. A cold shiver slithered down his spine. He shook his head, trying to get the thought out of his mind.

Ned turned away from the harbor toward the wooden, two-story building that housed Mama's Market, the younglings and others still close behind him. At one time, this building was the center of all harbor traffic. When the city grew, newer, larger buildings diverted traffic away from the old harbor. Now Mama's Market towered over mostly dust and shadows. Some of the stalls remained open, like the cobbler, but most had been abandoned.

The yellow paint on the facade of Mama's Market had faded on the wooden walls. Where it wasn't fading, it was either peeling or chipping. The planters between the first and second stories were mostly brown with only hints of green in them. Little white bugs floated around the nearly dead plants, looking for water and adding to the already desperate feel of the building.

Ned opened the left one of the double doors and reached down to unlatch the other. As he stood on two legs, it was difficult for him to find the latch. He ran his paws up and down the door, searching.

"You trying to scrape open my door? Hold your elk. I'll unlatch it for you," Mama, an old river otter, said from inside.

Mama's feet pattered across the wooden floor planks. The double doors swung open, and the intrusive spicy smell of pickled coral peppers caused Ned's eyes to tear up. He sneezed.

"Did you bring the entire city with you?" Mama nodded at the crowd that had followed Ned. "What does this lot want?"

"These fish." Ned held up the bundle. "Can I borrow some supplies?"

She shook her head and sighed. "Next time, try bringing me this many customers." She pushed past him and waved her gray paws to shuffle the crowd that had overtaken the entire street. "Step back. Step back. We're going to feed the lot of you. Gonna take me a moment to get set up." She pointed to a group of four otter younglings. "You four, grab some friends, and head to the beach or the forest. We're going to need some firewood. Then tell your parents to come get themselves a meal too."

The younglings ran off. Some of the adult creatures, who had joined the parade with their children, searched for a way to help. Mama pattered back into the market. When she looked back at Ned, she had a small grin.

"What should I do?" Ned asked.

"Everything. You're the fool who wanted to cook for the entire city."

Ned slumped and frowned.

"Don't give me that look." Mama grabbed some roots and vegetables from her shelves and glanced toward the back of the store. "Ivin!"

A dark-green iguana in a brown tunic scampered from the warehouse door. "Good to see you, Ned."

"Never mind him." She chuckled. "I need you to fetch those six large iron cauldrons and bring them out to the street."

"The street?" Ivin scratched his cheek as his tongue darted out.

"Yeah, the street. The bear here decided to cook for the entire city today."

Ivin raised an eyebrow and slowly went to retrieve the cauldrons.

Mama crossed her arms. "A lot of good he is. He's constantly having to hide. The whole world has gone mad. Those damn cats got everyone thinking the reptiles are the reason we're all poor. And he's too small to actually help me."

Ned smiled, knowing full well she adored Ivin. "You saved his life by giving him a job and a home."

"You're the one who found him fighting jaguars. Then you brought him here for me to feed and hide." She sighed. "I'm too tough on the hatchling. He's a good worker. Been a big help with my coral pepper sauce. Now, don't just stand there. Grab an empty salt barrel, and start shredding those fish."

Mama, Ivin, and Ned worked tirelessly at shredding fish, peeling roots, and chopping vegetables. With the additional help from some of the mothers from the horde, they were able to get all six cauldrons full of stew. The younglings had fetched plenty of wood, and the stew bubbled to the proper temperature. Creatures lined up with their plates, bowls, or boots, whatever they had that could hold the stew. Ned didn't care what they had—he ladled food into it. In one afternoon, Ned, Mama, and Ivin did what the golden cathedral couldn't do: they fed all those in Wexlin who wanted a meal.

"Thank you," Ned said to Mama after he carried the last cauldron in.

She huffed at him. "I thought you were coming here to ask for another recipe. If I'd known you were here to have me cook for you twice, I would've locked the door."

Ned chuckled. He had told her about the Sleeping Crawfish, and she had insisted that she and Ivin would go.

"They're going to walk all over you. You're a bear who won't smash the hive for the honey. We're going with you," she had said and refused to hear otherwise.

Ned knew better than to argue with her, and he was looking

forward to having the extra help. He didn't know what to expect tonight at the Sleeping Crawfish, nor did he know what to cook. He let out a big yawn and sat on the floor in the middle of the market. The day of fishing and cooking had finally caught up to him.

*I just hope I can stay awake.*

## Chapter 3
# The Sleeping Crawfish

The moon was high in the night sky by the time Ned, Mama, and Ivin reached the Sleeping Crawfish with their cart full of supplies. It was a modest wooden building alone at the end of the block just outside of the city, exactly where Tino had told him it would be. The inn's wood siding had been whitewashed to contrast with its dark-evergreen trim. A hand-painted sign depicted a crawfish sleeping in bed. Tino waited for them outside, clad in the same tattered clothing from that morning.

Ned wanted to flee. He suddenly lacked the desire to be there. *What did I get myself into?* He hardly knew these otters, and now he was going to be stuck with them in an unfamiliar place. He should have never brought Mama and Ivin. What if they were setting him up to press-gang him into military service? It had happened to him in bear country. It could happen to him here too.

"They thought you weren't coming. They kept telling me to start cooking, and I told them to wait. I knew you'd be here. And you brought help."

Mama wrinkled her brow but didn't say a word. Tino gave an awkward laugh and introduced himself to Ivin.

"I'll show you where you'll be cooking." Tino led them down the back alley of the Sleeping Crawfish. "Ned, how far along are you in that book you're reading?"

"About halfway through." Ned scratched his elbow. "I'm at the part where he's sliding down the snow hills with the penguins."

"Oh, I want to be able to do that too someday." Tino grinned. "That's about when he starts talking about Goran's gold, right?"

"No, he hasn't mentioned Goran yet."

Ned knew otters still prayed to Goran, the sea otter god of the oceans, but he knew nothing about his gold.

Mama scoffed and rolled her eyes. "Rubbish."

"What is it?" Ivin asked.

"It's the treasure of everything lost at sea," Tino said. "The one from the book Ned's reading."

"It's a story for fools and pups," Mama said. "That story has made more widows than fortunes. A buffoon's quest."

Tino tugged at his whiskers as if looking for something to say. Instead, he said nothing and led them through the double doors into the Sleeping Crawfish.

A large stone hearth was centered on the back wall, with two long tables occupying the middle of the room. On the opposite wall was a door large enough for Ned to squeeze through. *Must have been built for a crocodile. Nothing else that big would be around here.* He released a pent-up breath. He had worried he wouldn't fit through the door, an issue with most of the places he tried to visit in Wexlin. He wasn't surprised, as Wexlin was built for otters.

An iron, wood-burning stove caught his eye. It was made for otters but was large enough for Ned to make use of it. Thankfully, he could do the majority of the cooking over the fire. Ivin immediately began building a fire in the stone-arched hearth while Tino led Ned into the noisy lounge.

Ned squeezed his way through the door as the crowded room

fell silent. He clenched his jaw before his tongue could flop out. He could not stop himself from swallowing and trying to clear his throat. He tugged at the bottom of his shirt to make sure it covered his belly.

A simple rectangular table occupied the center of the room, and the eight creatures who occupied it locked eyes on Ned. There was an older beaver with small round eyeglasses, a crocodile, two river otters, two red foxes, and two creatures Ned had never seen before.

One of those creatures stood from the table. His fur was black except for strands of cinnamon that laid claim to the crown of his nearly square head. His chest was twice as broad as his hips. He wore a fine pair of navy-blue trousers and a matching seven-button vest over a modest yellow shirt. Based on a description from one of Labarre's books, this was a gorilla, the first creature from a distant land Ned had ever met.

"Jaja welcomes you." He laughed and approached Ned and Tino. "The chatty otter says you cook fish better than any of these merchants sail." He towered over Ned. "Stand up, bear. Don't be shy here."

Ned liked the idea of being able to stand. It would be like back home. Jaja's grin grew with Ned's height as he stood. Ned was a whole head taller than him.

Jaja let out a bellowing laugh. He bear-hugged Ned, picking him up off the floor and setting him back down. Ned's heart pounded, and he blinked rapidly. No one had picked him up since he was a cub.

"Let Jaja introduce you to some of our officers." Jaja placed his hand on Ned's shoulder and guided him over to the table. "You know our master gunner, Norbert."

Norbert tipped his mug to Ned and winked.

Jaja pointed to the smaller of the two red foxes. "This is our master of arms, Big Eli." He motioned to the other one. "And his cousin, our bosun, Lil Eli."

The larger and more muscular red fox nodded at Ned. Ned smirked at the larger fox being called the little one.

"The finest sailing master and carpenter you'll ever meet, Natty Nimbles."

A chubby beaver nodded.

"Our navigator and second mate, Kenson."

The crocodile stood and gave a slight bow.

"The captain's first mate, Guidry."

A stout otter with salt-and-pepper brown hair frowned at Ned.

"And our elected quartermaster, Amina." Jaja gestured to the dog creature Ned hadn't seen before.

"A quartermaster and a first mate?" Ned was hardly familiar with ship politics, but even he knew ships didn't typically have both.

"Ah, and the otters said you knew nothing about life at sea." Jaja chuckled. "They both received the same amount of votes from the crew to be quartermaster, so the captain gave them their titles and delegated the duties. Amina is a superb tactician but lacks basic social skills."

"My social skills are fine," Amina said. "It's the crew's incompetence that's the problem."

Norbert rolled his eyes at Ned. "See?"

Amina slapped the mug out of Norbert's paw. The tin tankard crashed to the floor, sending its contents spraying.

"You want to say something else?" Amina narrowed her eyes at Norbert.

"No, just going to go pour myself another drink." Norbert shook the liquid off his paw and pushed himself away from the table.

"Ned," Mama said from behind him. "Are you planning on helping, or should I just do it myself?" She pattered across the floor and stood in front of him and Jaja. "You talking or cooking?"

"I know you." Guidry stood on his chair and stared at her. "How do I know you?"

Mama snorted. "I've been in this city since before you were alive, stranger. You don't know me. You've likely seen me or purchased my pepper sauce." She grabbed Ned's paw. "Come on now. We've got plenty of work to do while this lot plots their next crime."

"No." Guidry stepped onto the table. "I know who you are." He glanced at the others, who didn't move. "You're with this bear?"

"No, he's not my type. Get your boots off the table. Other creatures are going to be eating there."

Guidry climbed down. "Do you plan on chartering a ship with this bear?"

"Otter, I don't have the slightest idea what you're referring to. I can hardly swim these days. I have no intention of going anywhere near the sea. Now, if you're finished." She tugged Ned's paw. "We've got work to do."

She led Ned away from the table and back into the kitchen.

"What was that about?" Ned asked.

"I haven't the slightest idea. It appears he's getting me confused with some other old otter he knows."

Ned didn't believe her, nor did he know how to press her further about it. He turned back around to find the entire table of creatures staring at them. He scratched his whiskers and frowned. Mama didn't seem bothered by the encounter and just chopped vegetables. *If she's not worried, why should I be?*

Ned took the salted pork out of the barrel and shredded it with his claws. Ivin shut the large kitchen door to silence the murmurs from the table, and the three of them, along with Tino, prepared the meal in silence.

* * *

Ned nodded and clapped while looking over the mess in the kitchen. It had been a job well done. He had served blackened catfish over wild rice and shredded pork with a side of roots and butter-soaked corn. He placed the pork on top of the rolls with a dash of his homemade sauce.

Water splashed over from Ivin filling the dish tub.

"Did you eat?" Ned asked.

"Later." Ivin returned to washing dishes.

Ned piled leftover portions of blackened catfish, smashed roots, wild rice, grilled corn, and shredded pork on top of a biscuit. He was more liberal with the spicy red sauce he had made from scratch on his own dish.

"Ned!" Jaja called from the other room. "Ned! You back there?"

Most of the crew had already left when Ned came through the door. Jaja waved him over. Only a sleeping Norbert, Jaja, Guidry, and Amina, who Ned had learned was a hyena from the same lands as Jaja, remained.

Jaja was the only one still eating. With his mouth full, he pointed at the almost empty plate in his other hand. "This is my eighth plate of this pork." He swallowed and smiled. "My favorite dish!" He shoveled more into his mouth.

Ned smiled. At least one of them enjoyed the pork.

"What part of the north do you come from, Ned?" Guidry asked.

"I'm not from the north." Ned took a bite. "I'm from the western coastal mountains along the Snake River."

"Ned, you must tell Jaja about your homeland, and Jaja must know how you made this sauce," Jaja said, chewing.

"Gladly." Ned took his own spoonful of food. "But I'm curious to know how you all ended up in Wexlin."

Tino rushed in from outside and stood on the table, swaying his mug. "'Tis a perfect evening for the tale of the greatest otter pirate captain to sail the known seas and beyond."

"Not for me it's not." Guidry pushed away from the table and rose.

"Fine. I'll let you tell the story, Guidry," Tino said. "Don't be a grumpy badger."

Guidry didn't reply. The door shut behind him.

Amina took one last sip from her tankard and stood. "I have also grown too tired. Tino, good fortune for you our meeting had adjourned before you came back in here." She gave him a side-eyed glance and left.

"Pay no attention to them." Jaja took a bite of pork. "Sour blood in the arms. Some wounds will always ache."

"Should I tell the story?" Tino asked.

"I'd like to hear it." Ned shoveled in another spoonful of pork. The texture had just the right amount of crisp and was accented perfectly with his spicy red sauce. He sighed in satisfaction and ate another bite.

Tino cleared his throat, acting reluctant to tell the story. He completed the charade by placing his empty paw behind his back and strutting across the table.

"Captain Elick Mandrin was Lord Mandrin before he ever stepped foot on the *Ironwill*. He was the second son of the Mandrin family, a very wealthy otter family here in Wexlin. The third wealthiest otter family from these parts. While his older brother spent his days grooming himself to become the lord of his land, the sea called to Elick. Elick commissioned his own sloop, and while on a voyage to Crocodile Island, his ship and his officers were taken prisoner by a foreign lion's pirate ship, the *Sharkbite*.

"The *Sharkbite*'s captain decided to sail to Wexlin and demand a ransom for his prisoners. Lions don't write in otter, so their captain called on Lord Mandrin to write his own ransom note. The *Sharkbite*'s captain asked for five thousand pieces of Wexlin silver. Elick laughed at him and said he didn't realize whom he had taken prisoner. Five thousand was an insult to the Mandrin name. He demanded they raise his ransom to twenty thousand pieces of silver."

"He raised his own ransom?" Ned widened his eyes as he

looked to each creature for an answer. "Why would anyone do such a thing?"

"It was the only way he could save his own life and the rest of his crew's. For that high price, Elick negotiated sending all his officers home with a note to his brother that read, *'Twenty thousand silver. Pay it. I'll retrieve it with interest.'* Elick told the captain it would take time to retrieve the coin and that the captain could exchange him whenever he wanted as long as they gave the Mandrin family thirty days to gather the silver. Their captain agreed to Elick's terms, sent away all of Elick's remaining crew, and kept him captive."

Jaja laughed. "He never acted like a prisoner. Mandrin was giving orders even when he was in shackles."

"That's my favorite part." Tino laughed. "He treated the pirates as his subordinates. When they asked him to do something, he delegated the job to the creature he saw more fitting to perform that task."

Jaja pointed with his spoon. "Jaja's favorite was when he recited poetry in the evenings. You wouldn't know this about Mandrin, but he has the voice of a bard. He sang the songs of his lands, and most of the crew found him amusing. Jaja thought he was magnificent."

Tino frowned. "I thought I was telling the story."

With a mouth full of food, Jaja waved his spoon for Tino to continue.

Anticipation curled in Ned's gut. He really wanted to hear more. It was outlandish that this otter prisoner was giving orders by day and singing songs by night. He'd seen prisoners before. They were locked in cages and never given more than a small bowl to use for everything.

Tino took a sip from his tankard. "But there were others who still referred to him only as the 'river rat.' Elick warned them they would be the first he'd kill when he came back for them. They just laughed, still believing he was their prisoner."

"Why did he hate being called a river rat so much?" Ned asked. "Seems hardly worth getting so worked up about."

"All river otters are called river rats because we're not like Goran's sea otters. We're their bastard cousins, and so other creatures think this name insults us. It did for a while until we embraced it." Tino took a long drink from his tankard and wiped the foam from his lips. "For thirty days, Captain Mandrin lived with the pirates, and Jaja was in charge of guarding him."

"Jaja was." Jaja laughed. "My old captain thought someone would kill him because he kept giving orders. That's when Elick and Jaja became friends. He saw things the way Jaja did."

Tino raised his voice. "When the thirty days were over, the ship left its island hideout and sailed back to Wexlin. Elick's officers were waiting at the docks in full military garb. When Elick handed over the chest filled with silver, he reminded the pirates he would make sail shortly and kill them all. The pirates laughed and sailed back to their island hideout."

"Three days after he returned to Wexlin, Captain Mandrin readied three ships with the promise to end the bloodshed on the water." Tino chuckled. "It's funny in hindsight. Anyway, Mandrin refused to fly the Wexlin banner. Instead, he had his own pirate flag made—a seated otter skeleton holding an hourglass with the sand running out. Gracefully warning all those who saw her, 'Your time is up.' Then he sailed southeast to seek revenge."

"This is when Jaja escaped from slavery." Jaja put his hand on Ned's back. "That's why Jaja is loyal to Captain Mandrin. He saved us from that lion who bought us and held us prisoner on that dreadful ship. We never saw our coin, so we could never leave his service. We wore all we owned."

"I haven't gotten to that part yet, Jaja." Tino spilled the remaining contents of his tankard as he placed his hands on his hips.

"Jaja apologizes. Please finish the story."

"You see, Ned, the *Sharkbite*'s pirates left their ship docked in the harbor with a small crew aboard. Under the cover of a moonless night, Captain Mandrin positioned his three vessels to blockade the pirate ship in the shallows. He waited till sunrise to open fire so all the pirates could watch it sink. The ship tried to fire back but stood no chance against three fully crewed galleons. Over the following two days, Captain Mandrin's ships bombarded the shore with cannon fire, destroying the little haven the pirates had created there."

Tino smiled. "The pirates raised a white flag. So Captain Mandrin and two hundred armed otters rowed ashore. The defeated pirate crew stood on the beach to meet their conqueror, most of them surprised it was the otter they had just let go. Captain Mandrin collected all his silver along with any other riches the lion captain had stashed away on the island. He took their captain captive and executed most of the crew right there on the beach."

"Jaja was hiding in the jungle with Amina and Calico. Mandrin said he'd spare Jaja and those Jaja trusted if we helped him. He even offered us a job on his ship. And here we all are nearly ten years later." Jaja laughed and saluted Tino with his mug.

"And this is the otter you now serve?" Ned asked. "The pirate hunter who became a pirate king? You're not free, Jaja. You merely traded getting orders from a different type of killer."

Jaja stood and dusted breadcrumbs off his vest. "Ned, we can only pray for the peaceful world you dream about, but this life will always be full of young creatures dying for old creatures' disputes. My suggestion to you is to find a lord or a captain or a king who sees the world the same as you. There will be less disappointment."

"I don't want to believe that's true," Ned said.

"Nor did Jaja." He sighed and looked out the window.

Another snore sounded. Tino had fallen asleep beside Norbert.

Jaja closed his eyes and shook his head. "It's a cruel world we live in. Jaja will help you load your cart."

He kicked the table. Neither Tino nor Norbert woke up.

Jaja rolled his eyes. "Jaja will have to carry these two home."

# Chapter 4
# The River Rat Summons

It was midday when Ned made his way to his job at the mine. He had overslept and was late. He'd have to work till after sunset to make up for the time he missed. The air was sticky, as it always was around this time of day, which was why the road was often deserted.

Jaja met Ned near the bend before the embankment and informed him he no longer had a job.

"What do you mean I don't have a job?" Ned asked, unable to control his panting. "You had no right to do that. Now how will I make coin to feed myself?"

"Jaja is sure the otter Bourg will let you back to work. He even said so. Jaja's brother Dingani is working for Ned today. He was most excited to do so. Dingani never cared for the sea, and when Bourg told him how much he would pay, he got to work with two pickaxes." He chuckled. "Don't be upset. It can be just for the one day or for however long you'd like. Come walk with me."

Ned slowed his panting and took a deep breath. *Who does this gorilla think he is, giving away my job? Even if it is just for the day. But why did he do it?*

They crossed over a small bridge onto Canal Street. Ned thought about jumping in to escape the heat. Memories of the citizens emptying their chamber pots into the slow-moving water made him cringe. *Perhaps jumping into the water is a bad idea.*

"Jaja told the captain about your food, and he would like to meet you. Jaja wants to show you our warehouse. You will be impressed."

Ned raised his eyebrows. "I've been in Wexlin for six moon cycles, and the city's occupants have cowered away from me like I would eat them if they came too close. It wasn't until I started feeding the younglings that they stopped running from me. Now you want to show me your valuables. Why?" He tilted his head away.

"How can Jaja convince you to sail with us on the *Ironwill*? Riches? Beauty? Adventure? What part would you like Jaja to tell you?"

"All of that would be wonderful, but I just don't think it's wise for me to get on a boat. We could all starve. There will never be enough food on a boat for my liking." He avoided telling Jaja the truth—he was too afraid of the ocean to board a boat.

"The crocodiles of Crocodile Island would teach you how to cook pork. And rice and beans. They make the finest rice and beans," Jaja said.

They arrived at an unassuming warehouse near the harbor. It was larger than Ned imagined. The building was a relic from when the crocodiles ruled over these lands. Like most crocodile buildings, there was no ramp or dock built on the nearby harbor. It was a long, whitewashed rectangle with a tarred, pointed roof and two green doors large enough for bison carts to enter. He frowned, the fur on the back of his neck prickling.

"Why aren't there any guards?" Ned asked.

"You wouldn't bite the hand that feeds you, nor would anyone in this city ever think to cross Mandrin. This is where the captain will meet you." Jaja pushed open one of the green doors.

They passed through a mob of river otters inside the warehouse. The ship's cargo had been unloaded here and was being sorted. Ned had never seen so much clothing, elegant furniture, exotic produce, and an abundance of grain all in one place before. Jaja guided him through the crowd toward a single room at the back of the warehouse, passing mounds of eyeglasses, watches, and gold-plated fur brushes.

A large painted oak table occupied the center of the room. Guidry stood on a stool at the far end of the table. Amina loomed over his shoulder. She placed her paws on the table as she studied a map.

The crocodile Ned briefly met the night before, Kenson, rolled up scrolls. He pulled away what Amina had been studying, rolled it up, and slipped it into a locked canister by itself. She snarled at him. Kenson motioned toward Ned. Amina looked at him and frowned.

"Just in time," an elegantly dressed otter said from the back of the room. "That's enough for today. Why don't you give me, Jaja, and Ned the room?"

The officers gathered their things with grumbles of displeasure and left.

"Welcome, Ned. My name is Elick Mandrin. Please." He motioned to a chair behind Ned.

Mandrin smoothed his green haretail jacket, then pushed up the long sleeves, exposing the frilled cuffs of his white shirt. He straightened and stared down his nose at Ned. Ned gulped. How did such a small animal command the room like that? He shrugged. Such a thing seemed common with wealthy, powerful creatures.

"Thank you for coming. My officers say we must have you on the *Ironwill* as our cook. We are an equal-shares ship, so you will be entitled to whatever plunder there is just like the rest of the crew."

"Why does the *Ironwill* really want me?" Ned asked.

"You should try Tino's cooking. Then you would understand our desperation." Jaja laughed.

"Agreed," the captain said. "We need a change in our galley. Even if you weren't a bear and were only half as good as Jaja and Guidry said, I'd offer you the same position."

"But because I am a bear?"

"Because you are a bear, you are invaluable to me." The captain smiled. "Ned, all types of creatures sail under my banner. On other ships, you'll find only otters or only crocodiles or only jaguars. But on the *Ironwill*, all are welcome."

"And all are welcome to leave when they want," Jaja said.

"From how you're looking at me, I can tell somebody told you the story of my revenge for my captivity. I was a younger otter and filled with rage. If I were to do it all over again, I'd do it differently."

"It makes no difference." Ned frowned. "You've become thieves. A lord and now a pirate, and you want to turn me into a pirate too. The penalty for piracy is death."

"You don't honestly believe that's all there is. Otherwise, you wouldn't be here talking to me." The captain leaned back in his chair. "Those of us you've met, you've liked. You're here because you don't want to think of your new friends as pirates. You want me to tell you we're not killers or thieves so you can justify your decision to join us. If we sailed under the Wexlin banner or the colors of some other ruler calling themselves a king, we'd be soldiers or privateers. We'd be heroes. Instead, you see us as criminals. Why? Because we don't fly the flag you like?"

"You justify being a pirate because kings start wars?" Ned said.

"No." Mandrin pulled at a thread on his shirt. "I mean to restore order to Wexlin. You haven't been here long enough to see how it's grown to become a city in ruin. Pirates control the bay, thieves control the streets, and this new southern jaguar hero church controls the governor. But you can't take control without coin, and I will never earn enough just farming the land of my estate."

"You want to rule Wexlin?" Ned stood, his nostrils flaring. He growled. "I've heard enough."

"Sit down, bear." A stern note in the captain's voice made Ned freeze. "You walked all this way. At the very least, you can let me explain everything before making your judgments. Besides, it's blooming hot out there. Have a cup of water, and listen to this otter ramble a bit longer."

Mandrin motioned for Jaja to retrieve some water and for Ned to sit. Ned glanced at the door. It would be easy for him to leave, but there was something about the way the captain sat in his chair, commanding and composed. Despite his better instincts, Ned sat.

"I understand how all of this seems sudden and suspicious to you." The captain took a cup from Jaja. "I'd be more concerned if you weren't suspicious. The truth is, Ned, I am the current ruler of Wexlin in all but name." He drank some water. "But I can't implement proper change from the harbor."

Ned accepted a large mug of water from Jaja, took a sip, and spat it out. "Ice-cold water?"

"Yes," the captain said through a grin.

"But how? There is no ice here." Ned's heart raced as he stared into his mug. "Poison?"

"Close. Alchemy. One of the many lost arts I wish to reintroduce back into Wexlin. The path of progress is through science and technology. I want to reopen the university and the shaman temple on the outskirts of town, where they will do more than just pray for the city like those jaguars."

"What about the cathedral?" Ned asked. "They won't be keen on the old ways coming back."

"Then I'll tear it down tower by tower, brick by brick, and sell each stone for grain to feed every empty belly if I have to. Until then, it can continue to remain useless in the center of the city."

Ned drank the cold water. He relished the way it washed over his dry tongue. It reminded him of home. He used to drink cool water from the stream every morning; it was the ultimate refreshment after a night spent sleeping with his mouth open. The air had been too cold then to indulge, but here in this warehouse where it was impossible to escape the heat, the cold water felt like a gift from the gods.

"I'm told you've read the works of Ulrich Leon Labarre," the captain said.

"He's not here for that." A tiger in a blue silk shirt that hung loosely off his orange fur emerged from the back shadows of the room. "He's here because of Maydia." He sat across from Ned. "They offer you a treasure hunt, but, my dear bear, you are the treasure."

"That's enough, Calico." Mandrin stood. "Ned, allow me to introduce you to our champion fighter, Calico Baco."

Ned had never seen a tiger before, but he had heard rumors about how big they were. Calico was twice the size of any jaguar or puma Ned had encountered. Calico muted the battle scars on his face with powder. Ned smirked. No matter how big Calico was, he was still a cat, and cats had always been so vain with their appearances. Bears wore their scars proudly as a sign of strength.

"What is a Maydia?" Ned scratched his knee. "Is that one of your gods?"

Calico snorted. "Only he sees himself as one. I can promise you this. If you seek Goran's gold, Maydia will seek you out."

The room had grown warmer, so Ned guzzled down the rest of his water. "What does Maydia want with me? I'm just an ordinary bear with no lands or titles."

"Labarre, Maydia, your gods' war, and the magic in these lands are all woven together like rope." The words purred from Calico's lips. "There is only one strand remaining—you."

"Me? How?" Ned's stomach turned sour, his throat too dry to talk.

Calico poured wine from a flagon. "They say a hundred thousand armored bears marched south to battle the gods and their armies, and when the armies were in ruin, the bear god stole the Land's power and wealth."

"Some say that," Ned said.

"What do the bears say?" Calico twirled his cup.

"Seek a scholar for a lesson in the histories if that's what you want." Ned crossed his arms. "I want to know who Maydia is, what he wants with me, and why."

"He's a myth." Captain Mandrin scoffed. "Another pirate legend."

Calico closed his eyes and took a deep breath. "He's hardly a legend, Captain." He stepped between Mandrin and Ned. "He's a powerful jaguar with a well-trained crew. Cursed to never step on land again. He seeks a bear to return the magic. Only a bear can bring back the magic to these lands. Tell me of your gods' war, and I'll tell you more of Maydia."

Ned rolled his eyes and sighed. "The gods and their lords grew greedy. They cast god stones into weapons and armor, creating armies of demigods. Bojana, the bear god, along with others, sought peace by disarming the mortal lords and bringing the stones back to the realm of the gods on Mount Porpra. Nobody willingly relinquishes power or wealth. The gods and their lords met in the center of the Land to destroy each other. Upon Bojana's request, ice bears, brown bears, and grizzly bears marched south, united for the first and only time."

"Do bears have mounts?" Calico asked.

"Young and small bears can ride a battle moose." Ned thought about his moose, Honor. He was proud of that moose and cried like a cub when it took a deadly spear blow in a battle. Now he was a full-grown bear at fifteen years and too big to ride anything. "Ice bears will ride mammoths, but most prefer elk chariots."

"This is why we're thankful the bear tribes fight each other and leave the rest of us alone." Mandrin peered around Calico. "We know the rest. The bears with Bojana marched south and overran the gods and their armies. What do the bears say about the lost magic?"

"When Bojana saw the death and destruction of the war," Ned said, "she decided to end it the only way she could. Legend says if a god forfeits their power, they are granted one final spell or wish. Bojana wished for all the magic and the stones to stop working. She threw her helmet in the river and vanished. Along with all the other gods."

"And the stones' power and all the magic vanished with her," Mandrin said. "Calico, we all know this tale."

"I still don't get what this has to do with me," Ned said.

"Everything." Calico's yellow eyes glowed in the candlelit room. "Labarre found Goran's treasure. It just so happens that Bojana's barbute was lost at sea. We find Goran's gold, we find Bojana's barbute."

Ned wasn't following. Bojana had thrown her bronzed helmet into the Muddy River, not the ocean.

Calico frowned. "You retrieve the barbute of Bojana, put it on, and reverse her curse. That will restore the magic in these lands. This is why Maydia needs a bear. He needs the magic to reverse the curse that has left him a prisoner on his own ship. And if you were to sail with us, he will find us. And when he does, I'm going to kill him. I'm going to kill the entire ship before we find Goran's gold."

"Calico, you'll frighten the bear with pirate stories." Mandrin stood. "If the curse is true and we draw the attention of Maydia, we'll be ready for him. As we always are."

"This time I'll have the moon steel." Calico brandished a sword with steel so white it glowed. It was the length of a longsword with a curved blade that broadened at the point. He slashed at the empty space in front of him, and the blade silently cut through the air. "Carved from a fallen star, this blade will kill even the immortals."

"You've seen Maydia?" Ned asked.

Calico sheathed his sword. "When I was a cub aboard my father's ship with a bear. A grass eater, a panda. The green sails of the *Dirty Whisker* towered over my father's schooner. Armored jaguars stormed the deck, took the grass eater, killed my father, and burned his ship. I escaped with my mother and floated on a barrel in shark-infested waters for three days. Listening to the screams of the other crew members being eaten alive. Just waiting for it to be our turn. Until a storm washed us ashore."

He kicked over a table loaded with scrolls and leather-bound books. The elegant furniture crashed to the floor, scuffing the dust off the stone.

Calico growled. "I was a cub, but I saw them. There is a ghost ship, and if Ned sails, it will come for us."

Calico narrowed his eyes at the captain, which sent a shiver down Ned's spine. Calico grabbed a flagon of wine, kicked over a chair, and stormed out of the room.

"Jaja will talk to him." Jaja followed Calico out the door.

Captain Mandrin hopped off the table and hovered over the scrolls and books scattered on the floor. He grabbed a particular scroll before returning to his chair.

"I'm sorry for Calico's behavior." Mandrin stroked his chin hair. "I believe Maydia is just a jaguar employed by the Southern Crown to scare us creatures of fortune. But a ghost ship? A captain and a crew forbidden to walk on land? Cursed to sail the seas, unable to die? It's absurd. Pirate tales. Walk into any tavern, and you'll hear a tale of five different ghost ships that haunt these waters. Sailors are a creative bunch when alone at sea. Perhaps I'm foolish, but the mind of a cub tends to broaden the truth."

Ned swallowed. "Captain, it sounds like Maydia has taken bears before, and it didn't work. Are you trying to get Bojana's barbute for yourself? You trying to become a god?"

Mandrin snorted. "Pirate tales." He took a long drink and placed the empty cup next to his feet. "I have found a map to Goran's gold, and only a bear can enter Goran's labyrinth. Together we'll unravel this world's greatest mysteries. Maydia, Bojana's barbute—I believe to be stories of legend. But Labarre found Goran's gold and left clues on how to retrieve it, and one of those clues is to bring a bear." He shifted his weight in his chair. "You wanted to know why you're invaluable to me, Ned? Because together you and I are going to solve Labarre's greatest riddle. Will you sail with me?"

"I won't. I won't help you start a war in Wexlin, nor do I wish to be on a boat."

"I know." The captain crossed his legs and placed his paws in his lap.

"You know?" Ned blinked rapidly. "If you didn't think I'd go, then why am I here?"

"To tell you of fate. You aren't here on my will or your will. The gods have brought you here. What are the chances that a bear would be in a city no other bear has visited with a captain who knows where Goran's gold is?"

Ned scoffed. "The gods didn't bring me here. I'm here because I want to be. I wanted to visit the city Labarre described in his books."

"Exactly. You may or may not know that Labarre's story, *The Land of Only Man*, was praised as one of the finest pieces of fiction written by an otter, much to his protest. The story of pale men living alone in rock cities was told to pups as a scary story. Labarre insisted his books were based on actual events. Creatures started to believe him after his book about the Sea Otter Islands, a place most could see or go visit. The nobles and scholars never accepted Labarre. It wasn't until he had been presumed dead that a ship of raccoons followed his map. The maniacs brought back a pale human female with golden hair and two of her offspring. I don't recall what became of the pale humans, but we discovered the tales written in Labarre's books were real." He chuckled. "Now they're the basis of all of our navigational maps."

Mandrin gave Ned the scroll he had picked up off the floor. It was Labarre's map of the world. The Land, shaped like a curled-up puma biting its foot, was centered, with a thin isthmus leading to the Land of the Barbarians. To the west, there was the three-pronged trident of the sea otter king on a crest over Cuwar Island, where Labarre famously swam in the blue lagoon and impressed the sea otters by diving to its bottom to retrieve a flat stone. Across the large Sunset Sea was a land mass Labarre had named the Land of the Striped Cat. South of it were scattered islands leading up to a larger island shaped like a paw pad and known as the Land of the Lizards and Roos.

East across the Sunrise Sea was the Land of Only Man. It circled part of the ocean with land masses that Labarre had carefully mapped out by sailing along the coast of the entire Swallowed Sea.

A bleak land mass called the Dark Lands, where Jaja and Amina were from, went unexplored by Labarre. He was sailing there when his ship was said to have been lost at sea. At the very bottom of the map was a circle with a tail land mass labeled the Island of Winter. In a small bay, there was a crest of a round, standing bird. It was the same crest on the book Ned was reading. Labarre had called the birds penguins.

Ned had seen this map many times but never with this much detail. Nor did it have the crest of Labarre's book covers on it. "Why are you showing me this?"

"It's a gift. Or a bribe. However you want to interpret it. Not everyone gets to own one of Labarre's paw-drawn maps. I know you will appreciate its value more than others."

Ned didn't know what to say. He was grateful, but he didn't want to take the map. He didn't want to be indebted to Mandrin.

"Take the map," Mandrin said. "All I ask in return is that you come speak to me again in two days' time. Until then, you won't hear from me."

# Chapter 5
# The Poet

Ned left the warehouse with a map and more questions. He thought about going to see Mama. She would know what to make of all of this.

Ned often wondered what his life would be like if he'd not been born a grizzly bear. He sometimes wished he was born a black bear. Black bears lived simpler lives. As nomads, they moved around in small tribes, going wherever destiny took them. They didn't make war. They didn't go into debt. And they ate plenty of food. *Only a brown bear or an ice bear would be stupid enough to change a system like that.*

He thought more about Captain Mandrin's offer. He'd be like a black bear. He'd have no taxes. He'd be part of a small tribe. He could fish off the side of the boat. All of it sounded wonderful, but he couldn't escape the fact that he'd be surrounded by hundreds of miles of open ocean. And now there was the lingering prospect of being hunted by a cursed pirate captain.

"Oy! Ned!"

Pierre leaned up against a tree beside the road. He effortlessly strummed a polished six-string lute with a wooden pick. When his song came to an end, he tipped his tricorn to Ned, grinning from ear to ear.

"What are you doing out here?" Ned asked.

"Waiting for you. I'm supposed to sit here and accidentally bump into you. Upon bumping into you, I'm to urge you to come with us on our next voyage."

"Why would you tell me that?" Ned asked. "The captain tell you to do this?"

"No. It was Jaja. As for telling you..." He played a tune. "I've never been any good at deception."

"How are you going to convince me to go sailing to the end of the world with a crew of otters and other creatures I don't know?"

"I'm not. Where are you headed?"

Ned raised an eyebrow. "I was going to go to the market, then back to my cabin outside the city. You're more than welcome to walk with me."

"Thank you. I will." Pierre strummed a tune as they walked. "The captain give you that map?"

"He did. Said it was drawn by Labarre."

"Likely. I know Guidry has been trying to get the captain to let him have it. Collectors would pay a lot of silver to get their paws on one of those. Captain never liked selling Labarre's stuff."

Ned looked at the scroll. "It was a nice gift, but I'm sure this one wasn't actually drawn by Labarre."

Pierre kept playing. "Have you held it up to the sun yet?"

"Why would I do that?"

"To confirm it's real. Labarre always put a secret message on his maps. Those maps are what started this treasure-hunting nonsense. That's why every wealthy otter wants one."

Ned stopped and studied the scroll. Could the map really have a secret message? Or would it be empty, confirming that the captain had given him a fake? He unrolled the map.

Pierre grinned. "Go on. I'm telling you, it's a real one."

Ned held the scroll up to the sun. The afternoon light blasted through the parchment. He squinted and frowned. He didn't see any writing.

"Give it here. Your bloody paws cover up half the map." Pierre took the map and held it up. "Here it is. Do you see it?"

Ned sucked in a breath. There was writing in the upper right corner. He couldn't read it. He tried slouching to look up at the map, but he was too tall. He decided to lie on his back while Pierre held the map over his face. He could easily read it now.

> *I alone had made it there*
> *To the land of treasures bold*
> *My path will show you where*
> *To make a new world from the old*
> *Journey south until it's north*
> *Tucked in ice you'll find a jungle there*
> *Alone you cannot go forth*
> *The key is a sleepless bear*
> *Take the bear on a turtle's back*
> *To marvel at my life's quest*
> *For riches too grand for any sack*
> *In success all shall be blessed*

"What does that mean?" Ned asked.

"It's a route to the treasure. All the main things we know are mentioned." Pierre pointed at the poem's lines to emphasize his points. "Land of treasures bold, he's talking about the treasure. The key is a sleepless bear, that's you. Journey south until it's north, that's this spot right here." He pointed to the penguin crest. "He mentions his compass doing that in this book. You see? It's all right there."

Ned mouthed the words as he read the poem over and over. He was trying to remember it all. *If it is really that easy, why hasn't anyone found it?*

His ears perked up when Pierre broke the silence to sing and play an upbeat tune.

*"This is a tale of an otter so brave, a place with the treasures of the deep.*
*From ships he buried under his waves, your gold is now Go-ran's to keep.*
*The blackfish are his eyes and his keepers. They're the ones to notify those he sires.*
*They tell him of the riches of sunken ships, all to be brought back to his massive island of fire."*

"What is that you're singing?" Ned asked.

"It's called 'Master of the Sea.' It's really popular around here. Do you want me to stop?"

"No, I like it. I've very much enjoyed hearing music played throughout the city."

"If you want to hear mediocre music, go to a castle. You want to hear music with heart, head down any alley in the city. Here, you're going to love the chorus of that song."

There was a bounce in Pierre's step when he sang and a smile that took over his entire face.

*"Go-ran, Go-ran, master of the sea. Pay him homage, and he'll let you be!*
*Fears only one, but you would too. It's Bo-jana the bear!*
*Bo-jana the bear. Black and brown, truly wise and fair.*
*Strong and powerful, and that's just her glare.*
*Bojana the bear is coming for you. And there is nothing Go-ran can do!"*

Pierre jumped and spun around to emphasize the end of the chorus. Ned laughed and turned down the old Main Street to the corner of Harbor where Mama's shop was.

"You sure can play that lute better than anyone I've ever seen. Aye, here we are." Ned pointed at Mama's Market.

"This place?" Pierre yelped and took a step back. "You come here? They say she's a witch."

"Mama? The old otter who runs the place?"

"Is that what she has you call her? She's the Wailing Widow."

"The Wailing Widow? What is that?"

Pierre pursed his lips. "She's the one who sank Labarre's ship. One of the last witches from a forgotten era. They say a sorceress stole Labarre away from her. After he left with the sorceress, she would walk to the water's edge, casting spells, wailing in the wind. Then one day, she stopped going to the beach, and Labarre was declared lost at sea. Never heard from again. To stay alive, she feeds off young otters who enter her shop."

Ned struggled not to laugh. This was a ridiculous rumor that any creature who spent any time with Mama would know to be false. "Pierre, I assure you, she's not a witch. She's just some old otter. Besides, if she is who you think she is, then she'll be the one to make the most sense out of this poem." He gestured to the map. "Come on. I'll show you."

Pierre shuffled his feet and drifted away from the door. Ned grabbed his arm and ushered him through the double doors into Mama's Market.

"Aye! What is this?" Pierre said. "It's a poison, some sort of potion. My eyes, my nose. What is this?"

Ned patted his back. "It's just coral peppers and salt. Try to sneeze, and it will go away."

"What's all the commotion out here?" Mama slowly walked in from the other room.

Pierre hid behind Ned.

"It's nothing." Ned nudged Pierre, who was rubbing his eyes. "I was going to get some more pepper sauce, and I wanted to ask you about this." He held up the scroll.

Mama took the scroll and moved behind the counter. She

unrolled it and only briefly glanced at it before letting it go so it could roll itself up.

She sighed. "Where did you get this? From the same pirates we cooked for? What do they want with you, Ned?"

Ned slumped and found himself fumbling the words. Pierre elbowed him and poked his head out from behind Ned's legs.

"Um, yes and no. Yes, the same pirates, but their captain gave me the map, and he wasn't there the other night."

"What do they want with you, Ned?" She pulled a note from her apron and held it up at Pierre. "Is this part of your doing too?" She opened it. "Our sincere gratitude for such a fine meal. Please use this coin to help feed those who are hungry or for whatever you deem fit. Truly yours, Captain Mandrin." She narrowed her eyes at Pierre.

"I know nothing about that." Pierre's voice shook. "We just want Ned's help finding Goran's gold."

With a frown, Mama hobbled toward the worn wooden stairs that led to the small room built in the rafters. "You two, start loading up the cart with the list of supplies I gave Ivin. I'll be right back."

Ned and Pierre shrugged at each other. Ned decided he would walk to the back and find Ivin. Pierre started playing "Master of the Sea" again, only this time it was more docile and his singing was more of a whisper.

> *"When Bojana saved us from external darkness,*
> *That bear had watched it all.*
> *She saw mighty empires finally fall.*
> *So she took the magic that destroyed us.*
> *She took that magic and tossed it into the sea.*
> *Still the greatest sacrifice was made by she.*
> *She removed her barbute, the source of all her power*
> *And every bear will argue this was perhaps her finest hour.*

*There were no laws to find the right paws. So she threw it in the river."*

"Are you singing?" Ivin popped up from behind a barrel.

Pierre flinched, and his lute made a small screeching noise. "Um, yes."

"Can you teach me that song?" Ivin's tongue darted out.

"I could, or I could teach you others." Pierre scratched his neck. "It's sort of an otter song, but the chorus is a lot of fun." He played the chorus with the same enthusiasm as if he had been playing to an audience of two hundred and not just Ivin and Ned.

"What is all this commotion?" Mama pattered in as Pierre finished. "Sounds like a pack of pups crying in here."

She slid a bundle in front of Ned. Books and scrolls spilled out onto the floor. Ned picked up one of the books and studied it. The cat on the seal looked like Calico. He ran his paw pads over the cover to clear the dust off the soft brown leather.

"Why are you giving me these?" he asked.

"So you have all of them to read. Sounds like you'll be out on the water and will need things to read. I could never bring myself to read it all. He left his journals and some drawings. I never could make sense of it, so I just hid them."

Pierre thumbed through a book. "So you did know Labarre?"

Mama bit her lip and looked away. She dusted her paws off on her apron before wiping a tear from her eye. "I knew him, yes. I used to run a small printing press when I was younger. A beaver sold it to me for just a silver. My father thought I was a fool, and perhaps I was until I met Ulrich. He told me a wild tale about how he had escaped from pale humans in a city of stones and rocks. It was fascinating, and when I told him about my printing press, we developed his tale into a book." She grabbed the cedar-brown leather book with the human hand on it and opened it in the middle. "We didn't really know what we were doing at the time or what really made a good story. I also hadn't noticed all the small letter *a*'s were backward. Seems that beaver sold me some faulty tiles." She handed Ned the book.

Ned laughed a little when he saw the errors. "Why didn't you tell me you knew Labarre?"

"I didn't want to get you involved in all this nonsense. I took no pleasure in seeing your nose in our books. But he didn't listen to me, so why would you? I told him it was all foolish. A bear going sailing on the riddle of an otter. It's absurd. What grand treasure he discovered did him very little good in the end."

"Goran's gold is real?" Ned's insides vibrated. He thought Mandrin had been telling him a tale to get him on his ship, but to hear it come from Mama was the confirmation Ned needed. His grin grew as wide as his face. "Can an ordinary bear like me really bring back magic?"

Mama looked down at the bag of books, then up at Ned. "Ulrich seemed to think so. He was obsessed with it. Said the gods had sought him out to restore their place in our world." She rolled her eyes and shook her head. "That's why he went to all these places. He was trying to bring back magic. Trying to find wizards or witches to bring back the old ways."

"He found a sorceress in the barbarian lands, didn't he?" Pierre leafed through a different book.

"He did. A giant otter." Mama approached the counter.

Ned put down the book and walked over to the map. "Did Labarre tell you anything about the poem he hid on his maps?"

She chuckled. "He fancied himself such a poet. It was supposed to lead creatures to his tomb. He liked the idea of fellow explorers coming to visit him. I don't believe he ever had one built. When you've been lost at sea, they tend not to build a tomb for you."

"Are you certain he was lost at sea?" Pierre asked. "His ship, the *Pelican*, was said to be magical, from a foreign world, and unsinkable."

"If he wasn't lost at sea, then he was lost in whatever adventure he found himself in." She threw roots into a sack. "If he was alive, he would've come back. He had an estate and a small fortune here. He wouldn't have left it all behind. Are we finished yapping about this? You're supposed to be back here helping Ivin, but instead, you're singing and interrogating me."

"Is there anything else you can tell us about the poem?" Pierre held the map up to a window for the light to shine through it.

"No. I told him he sounded foolish, going around telling everyone he was on a quest from the gods. He would discredit all his work." Mama sighed. "He wouldn't discuss it with me after that."

Ned wanted to know more, but he wasn't sure he could pry information from her. Discussing Labarre had made Mama more reserved. She stared at her empty paws before looking back at Ned with a hollow smile.

"Do you remember anything he said?" Ned asked.

She gave him a weak grin, tears brimming in her eyes. "Of course I remember things he said. I don't know much more about this poem. Rich otters have been coming in here for decades, asking me what it means, and I'll tell you what I told them. The books were his life's quest and part of a puzzle he saw something in that made him believe a bear was the key to getting the treasure. You have to sail to the snow island from his book. That's where he said Goran lived and where Bojana's barbute and countless other relics were. He also said he had the treasure map hidden on his ship. All someone needs to do is find his ship."

"No one has seen his ship in nearly thirty years," Pierre said.

"Forty-two years," Mama corrected. "You should forget all this, Ned. Go back home. I'm certain your mother misses you."

Ned frowned. He did miss his mother. Even his father and sister, who likely didn't miss him at all. By now they all knew he was a deserter, and his father would be doing everything in his power to erase the memory of a son who had betrayed and dishonored him. His litter mate, Ruby, a fine warrior, would've done the same. Or she was currently tracking him to kill him to collect the bounty for his desertion. The thought of his father and sister soured his stomach. He could never go back home. He just wished he could've told his mother goodbye. He knew she would always love him no matter what he did.

"I can never go back. But maybe if I found Goran's gold..." Ned shook his head. "Maybe not. Bears hate magic."

"They have always feared it," Mama said. "Bears think it's for the weak, yet they have not read the histories of our world with magic. There was no hunger or poverty. Kings ruled honestly. Cities were built with grand wonders that stand even today. Now little pups die in the streets while others walk over them. Many have fallen, and the gods haven't been there to save us. Greed is always the cause of a creature's undoing."

"What should I do?" Ned asked.

"You should stay. But not because I say so. You must decide what's best for you. Read those books, and see if the answer reveals itself. First, take this cart with supplies to the cathedral. Those priests have been harassing me for a donation, and this ought to cover it. If a pirate insists on giving me his blood money, I'm going to put it to good use."

She gave Ned the list of supplies and pulled his large paw close. She rubbed his fur and smiled before she pattered away.

"I'm tired," she called back to them. "See that you lock up when you leave."

# Chapter 6
# The Cathedral

The candles in the street lamps radiated the strong glow of being newly lit. The Wexlin streets were busy, as most otters preferred to be active at night. Market stalls opened, with their owners proudly displaying their goods at the prospect of a new night's sales. Otters dined on fine shellfish in the balconies of taverns, while Ned pushed the cart loaded with sacks of roots, vegetables, and beans.

He had been so lost in thought earlier about how Mama knew Labarre and that he could possibly bring back the magic that he had paid very little attention to how he loaded the cart. The salt barrels of fish and crawdads wobbled on every cobblestone, while the flagons of water and apple cider rolled from side to side, making it more difficult for him to push.

Ivin walked with him, doing his best to help push the cart, but he simply lacked the strength for Ned to notice if he was pushing or not. Pierre played his lute alongside the cart, drawing even more attention to them. They received a mixture of smiles and cheers for Pierre's music. Others shot them cold glares, as Pierre had told him that some thought the song to be cursed. A few even tossed coins his way. When they turned onto Royal Street, Pierre stood on top of the cart, singing to the busy evening's traffic. Ivin moved closer to Ned, his eyes darting back and forth.

"Oy! It's them!" Tino stood on the corner by a small tavern. "I told you we'd find them."

A large sea otter with facial scars stumbled out of the door, dragging a sleeping Norbert by his collar. With his other paw, he saluted Pierre with a tankard.

"Pleasure to see you out with the likes of us, Luka." Pierre dipped his lute to him.

"Even I need a night to forget now and then." Luka's deep voice bellowed into laughter. "Who's the lizard and bear?"

"That's my mate Ivin. And the big fella is Ned," Pierre said.

"Pleased to meet you both." Luka yawned. "Where you headed?"

"To deliver goods to the cathedral," Ned said. "Would you like to join us or—?"

"I'll join ya, Ned." Luka dropped Norbert, who hit the ground with a thud. "Let me just fix this. Looks like the road wobbled the haul loose."

Luka restocked the cart so its contents wouldn't wobble. When he finished, he threw a sleeping Norbert onto the sack of roots and helped push the cart. Ned nodded at him, thankful the cart was now significantly easier to push.

Luka returned the gesture. "Pierre, how about you sing us 'Master of the Sea' until we get there?"

Pierre jumped back on top of the cart. "Only if you sing the last bit with me. You know how much I appreciate our harmony."

"You don't have to ask me twice." Luka smiled and cleared his throat.

Pierre's grin was as wide as his face when he started playing. Even only being the second time Ned had heard it, he found it incredibly catchy, so much so he tapped his claws on the cart along to the beat. Luka, Tino, and most of the otters nearby joined Pierre to sing the chorus. When it was time, Pierre smiled and nodded at Luka. Luka closed his eyes, and with a beautiful, smooth, stony singing voice, he sang the final verse.

*"I wish that was the end of this tale.*
*But that Otter was tricky down to his core.*
*He sent those blackfish out on a hunt*
*To find the barbute the bear had worn.*
*There was no resistance on any front*
*Now that barbute is on the Otter's rocky ocean floor!"*

Pierre hooted and rolled his tongue into a scream of joy. Tino, Pierre, Luka, and just about everyone nearby on the street sang the final chorus in perfect harmony.

*"Go-ran, Go-ran, master of the sea,*
*Pay him homage, and he'll let you be!*
*The otter fears no one.*
*Bo-jana the bear, her power is done.*
*Bojana the bear,*
*Black and brown, truly wise and fair.*
*Strong and powerful, and that was just her glare.*
*Bo-jana the bear is coming for you*
*But there is nothing she can do!*
*There is nothing that bear can do!"*

All the otters erupted in cheers and whistles when it was over. Pierre bowed, waved, and started playing a softer tune as Ned and Luka pushed the cart through the gate of the statue garden of the cathedral.

A horde of creatures camped in the courtyard, lying among the bronze statues that held their paws over the desperate crowd. One by one, they lifted their heads to stare at them. Jaguars, pumas, red wolves, ocelots, margays, river otters, beavers, skunks, coyotes, and bobcats all lived together. A ravenous look in their eyes, their tongues lolled out. Several growls pierced the air, sending a shiver down Ned's spine. His heart pounding, he ran a hand along the back of his neck and tried to choke down his nausea. He shared a look with his companions as he pushed the cart toward the locked entrance of the cathedral. He wanted to give the food to the horde, but it needed to go to the priests so they'd stop sending guards to Mama's and demanding a donation from her. Now they were in trouble.

"What do we do now?" Ned said, trying to keep his voice from shaking.

"I know how to deal with this lot." Luka rattled the steel gate.

"Stop," Ned said.

"Father Moster!" Luka said.

The mob crept toward them. There was a loud creak as the cathedral's wooden door opened. The torchlight from inside flooded the courtyard, keeping the horde from advancing.

An old jaguar in white-and-gold robes scowled at them. "What is it?"

"Aye, Father Moster. It's me, Luka. We have a cart of donations."

"It's from the otter who runs the coral pepper market," Ned said.

Father Moster came forward and eyed the cart. "What do you bless the good lords with?"

"Just rations of food. I was hoping for some assistance for us to distribute it to your followers," Luka said. "We'd need some tables, some bowls, and some—"

"Yeah, yeah. Let's wheel it in." Father Moster unlocked the gate.

"Father, the rations are ready to go." Luka frowned. "Send one of my friends to fetch the cart I brought yesterday, and we'll hand it all out tonight. These creatures are hungry."

"That's not what we do. We'll decide when we'll hand it out. Now wheel it in."

Ned grabbed the gate. Father Moster froze. Ned smelled his fear, but the old cat puffed his chest out.

"What are you going to do, bear? Hit a sworn servant of the gods at the gates of their place of worship?"

Ned snarled. He didn't believe the priest was giving out the food. "Where is the other cart?"

Father Moster narrowed his yellow eyes. "Wheel the cart in, bear."

Ned tried to steady his breathing. He wanted to hit Father Moster. He took a couple of deep breaths. "You're not giving this food to them, are you?"

"What we do with donations is the Cathedral of the Oak's matter. Now, you and the otters wheel this cart in. That lizard is not welcome in the house of the gods."

Ned looked over at Ivin, who shrugged.

"Fine," Ned said.

Father Moster gave a victorious grin.

"Luka and I can handle this. I'll meet you all back at the shop. Hurry," Ned said.

Tino grabbed Norbert and hurried the others out of the plaza.

"I knew you'd come to your senses, bear. Foreigners and reptiles, they're a plague. The Land could do without any more of those. Follow me. Lock the gate behind you."

Father Moster turned his back to the cart. Ned narrowed his eyes and cocked his head at him. Luka cracked his knuckles and winked. Ned pushed the cart through, and when he cleared the gate, he rammed the cart into Father Moster's back, knocking him to the ground. Luka climbed over the cart to jump onto the scrambling jaguar's back. Luka did his best to keep Father Moster down while Ned jammed the cart in the entryway, propping the protective gate wide open.

"Luka, let's go!" Ned said.

Luka climbed back on top of the cart and tossed a heavy sack onto Father Moster's legs, who was trying to crawl away. The priest roared in pain.

"Creatures!" Luka called to the horde. "I bring food and supplies! There are enough riches in this building to save you all. Take it!"

The crowd hardly hesitated, leaving little time for Ned and Luka to get away. Ned and Luka ran toward the harbor as the swarm charged the cart. Ned never looked back, but he heard the mob make its way over the cart and into the cathedral. He stopped hearing Father Moster's roars when they exited the plaza.

Ned struggled to catch his breath. "What did we do?"

"I don't know. I knew they weren't giving those creatures any of the food we have been giving them. They'll have us killed for this. What now, Ned?"

"We find the others and hide from the Wexlin city guard."

This wasn't what Ned had intended. He just wanted to feed the hungry again. Now he had started a riot. After this, there was no way he could walk through the city. The city guard would demand justice.

# Chapter 7
# The Escape

Ned woke with pain in his lower back and in the back of his throat. The memory of the riot from the night before played in his head over and over. He had spent the night pushing over trees, and when he got tired but couldn't sleep, he destroyed the walls of his cabin until he collapsed on the floor. The horde of creatures that had been camped among the statues ransacked the cathedral, dragged twenty holy jaguars out of their quarters, and executed them among those same bronze statues. All Ned wanted to do was help Mama.

Lord Ludwig Clayborn, the governor of Wexlin, dispatched his entire royal guard to retake the cathedral and gather those they deemed responsible. They had shown up at Mama's in full green-plated sharkskin armor, looking for Ned, knowing that was a place he frequented. She told them nothing, and Ivin snuck out in the heat of the midday sun to warn Ned that they both had bounties on their heads.

Ned's first thought was to head west to find a cooler place on the coast to live, but there was Ivin. Ned had gotten him into this mess, and now Ivin had no place to go.

Ned sent him ahead to tell Jaja they would sail with the *Ironwill*. When a day had passed and Ivin had not returned, Ned expected the worst. It wasn't until sunset that he saw a familiar otter heading toward his cabin.

"Oy!" Pierre said. "A real mess we got ourselves into."

"Where's Ivin?"

"Aboard the *Ironwill* by now. Was easy getting him out of the city. We needed to think about what to do with you."

"And?"

"And nothing for now. Pack a bag, and bury what you can't bring. We leave in the morning."

"What will you do?"

"Catch up on some sleep before we sail." Pierre lay on the porch bench, placed his tricorn over his face, and went to sleep.

Ned shoved what he could into his leather pack. The clothes he wore now would be what he wore for perhaps the next year, with the exception of a few extra garments he was able to stuff into his pack. He tightened the belt on his black breeches and put on a clean long-sleeved white haretail shirt that made his neck itch. He stretched out the collar and scoffed. He hated wearing a shirt. Before he put on his boots, he stared at them and thought about how much ground they had covered together from his home. Now he would walk on faraway lands with them.

He loaded all of Labarre's books into a separate satchel along with the scrolls, loose parchment, and journals Mama had given him. When he had packed everything he needed, he tried to sleep. He kept looking out the window, afraid he'd miss the sunrise. He would remember something else he wanted to pack and immediately get out of bed to add it to his things. Tears welled in his eyes as he held the blade sharpener his mother had given him. He wiped his nose and stuffed the sharpener into his bag. His sour stomach kept him awake, which allowed him to pack every gift from his mother. He knew he was likely to never return here.

The sun peeked over the horizon, waking Pierre. Ned hadn't

slept. Yet he was not tired. He threw his bags over his shoulders and headed outside. When he closed the door to his small cabin, he couldn't help but run his paws over the doorframe. This had been the first house he had ever built for himself.

"It will be all right," Pierre said. "We'll only be gone a couple of months. Things will have died down, and you'll be able to come back."

Ned frowned. They walked in relative silence. Ned slowed at every crossing to peek around the corner, expecting to find a platoon of soldiers waiting for them.

"You should've brought me a weapon. How do we get there without the guards seeing us?" Ned asked.

Pierre laughed. "You are the weapon. We're taking the long route. It's morning time, so there won't be enough out on patrol to see us. You'll see."

They crossed over the northern bridge of the canal. Guards emerged from the forest. Ned turned to run, but six jaguars with shields and spears blocked their retreat. They were surrounded. Ned searched for some sort of weakness and counted helmets. *Twenty-two. No, twenty-five, no, six. That might be too many.*

"Why don't you own a weapon?" Pierre pulled his pistol and sword.

"There will be no need for that." Lord Gallant in full sharkskin armor rode his young elk past the shield wall in front of Ned. "Surrender and we'll be merciful. Fight and you will die. Slowly."

"May we offer different terms?" Pierre asked.

Lord Gallant laughed. "You are hardly in a position to offer terms. See what happens when you get mixed up with this bunch, bear? I offered you coin and power, and now you'll rot as a slave. Waking up every morning, wishing you had made a different choice. Come quietly." He tossed iron shackles at Ned's feet.

"Are those for you? All I smell is fear, and all I see are dead jaguars." The odds were against him, but Ned knew not to show his enemy any doubt. Besides, they didn't know what he was capable of.

Lord Gallant snorted. "You will rue the day you crossed the otters of Wexlin. Now, put on the shackles, and come with me."

Ned picked up the shackles and ran a claw over the chain. "I offer new terms. We leave Wexlin, and everyone here goes home alive and uninjured."

Lord Gallant raised his eyebrows before breaking into laughter. "Can you fly, bear? Don't make us kill your friend in front of you."

Ned whispered to Pierre, "How far is it?"

"Two miles."

"What are you two whispering about? Surrender now." Lord Gallant waved the guards forward.

Ned sighed. They weren't going to be able to outrun them, and he was outnumbered nearly thirty to one, with an ally armed with just one pistol. He was going to have to fight his way out of this, and he didn't have a weapon.

Ned rolled up the shackles and threw them at Lord Gallant, which knocked him off his mount. The young elk reared, kicked, and scattered the shield wall as Ned hoped. Ned growled and charged forward. He scooped up the dazed Gallant and tossed him into the shield wall.

Ned punched his way through the fractured ranks. They managed to pierce through, but it was still too far to run.

Pierre jumped onto Ned's shoulders to reload his pistol. "East harbor."

Ned backpedaled away from the city guards as they reformed their ranks. It was less than half of them, as some tended to the injured or had lost interest in pursuing a bear. Ned stood tall and gave a mighty roar. The guards tossed a large net over them.

The stones weighed them down, and Ned and Pierre were entangled. *Why is it always nets?* Nets were a common tactic when fighting a bear. Ned put his paws into the same square and ripped off the net. Pierre fell to the ground.

The soldiers tossed two more nets on top of him. *Don't panic. Remain calm.* Remembering his training, Ned grabbed the stones and peeled the two nets off him and Pierre. A jaguar leapt on Ned and plunged his claws into Ned's back. Ned roared in pain. The soldier went to stab him, but Ned bucked backward, causing the cat to drive his dagger into Ned's pack instead. Ned fell backward, crushing the jaguar under his weight. Blood trickled down his back from the jaguar's claws.

The city guard inched forward. Pierre fired his pistol over Ned's shoulder. With a roar, a soldier dropped his spear and grabbed his wounded arm.

Ned growled. "Not near my ear."

Ned sneezed and shook his head to shake the humming out of his ear. He gathered himself and kept backpedaling, waiting for the next one to advance or for some sort of advantage. The city guard moved their shield wall forward, maintaining their distance from Ned. Pierre fired the occasional shot, but he hit mostly shields.

They tossed another net, this one falling short, but it was meant to be a distraction. Two guards charged them. Ned parried one spear and grabbed the second. Pierre countered with his sword, and the jaguar threw him to the ground. Ned kicked him before he could deliver the final blow to Pierre. The other jaguar swiped at Ned with his dagger, ripping through Ned's shirt. He had caught his fur but not his belly. Ned punched him in the face but caught more helmet than flesh. He winced and shook his paw. The two jaguars were shaken but quickly rejoined their ranks. Pierre fired his pistol into the shield wall.

"You got any ideas?" Pierre's paws shook as he reloaded.

Ned laughed. He saw the advantage he needed. "We're going to get out of this." He pointed at a stack of stones used to continue a wall of some noble's estate.

Pierre frowned. "How? By waiting for them to finish building the wall?"

Ned rolled his eyes. He darted over to the pile of stones and grabbed one from the top. It was smooth and a little bigger than his paw pad. He flipped it to get a better grip. Perfect weight. He hurled it at the advancing shield wall.

The stone hit a shield with enough force that it knocked the jaguar off his feet. Ned had already thrown a second one before they could close ranks. The rock caught a corner of the shield, splintered the wood, and hit the jaguar in the face. He let out a wounded roar before retreating.

Ned held a stone in each paw. He bared his teeth and growled. The much smaller shield wall regrouped and proceeded to retreat. Ned let out a roar to encourage them to move faster. Pierre fired and struck one of the soldiers who had fallen out from behind the wall.

Pierre reloaded. "Time to run?"

Ned heaved a stone at the shield wall. It shattered a shield and sent the ranks into a scattered retreat.

"Now is good." Ned dropped the second rock, and they ran toward the east harbor.

Pierre laughed. "You defeated an entire regiment without taking off your packs."

Ned grinned. "They weren't fighters. Just big cats trying to make easy coin." He blew out a breath. *We got lucky.*

Ned followed Pierre through the city to the harbor. It would be harder for them to be taken by surprise with the daily city traffic. His shirt stuck to his bleeding back. His wounds didn't hurt nearly as much as his paw did from hitting the helmet. His fingers throbbed and started to swell. They took the east road out of Wexlin to the harbor.

Tino and Norbert waited for them at the end of a small wooden dock comprised of red cedar trees split in half and tied together. The flat side of the split tree was for walking on, while the round side, often still with branches attached, rested on the wooden barrels. The dock had a mere eight support beams anchored into the muddy waters in the shallows of the cove. Pierre ran over the bridge, threw supplies into the boat, and frantically barked at the others.

Furrowing his brow, Ned took a few tentative steps toward the otters. The trees buoyed and swayed under his weight. He paused to steady himself. The water rose between the planks. The dock was sinking. His heart leapt, and he instinctively retreated back to shore. *This is a mistake. What was I thinking? Bears are too big to be sailors. The dock sank. No way that little boat will float when I get in. I'd rather fight the jaguars.*

"Ned, you have to keep moving. It won't sink as long as you keep moving," Tino said.

Ned didn't believe him. His knees trembled, and he was reconsidering his decision to come. He'd leave Wexlin tonight. He could easily find a job in another city. Maybe he could head back west and live among the pumas in the mountains as far away from the ocean as possible.

"They're coming. Hurry!" Pierre pointed at the soldiers in the distance.

*You can do this. Worst case, you'll fall into a couple feet of water and swim to shore.* He knew how to swim. He tentatively placed his booted paw back onto the floating red cedar. It gave a little, but he kept walking, fast at first until he got comfortable enough to walk normally. After a few steps, he rather enjoyed it. It was like walking on air.

"Step into the middle of the boat, and steady yourself as quickly as possible." Tino held the ropes to a four-benched rowboat alongside the dock.

Ned stepped right into the boat. It swayed and nearly tipped. He grabbed both sides to steady himself and slowly sat on the center bench. The boat continued to buoy up and down, smacking against the side of the wooden dock until the otters pushed off. They took turns jumping in, barely affecting the boat's movement.

Pierre sat across from Ned. "We thought you'd tip the boat."

Norbert and Tino retied the ropes in front. When they were

done, they tossed the loose ends into the water. There were no oars in sight. Ned wasn't sure how they were going to get to the ship.

"Ready now, Vesna! Luka!" Tino called out into the harbor.

Norbert and Tino took their seats next to Pierre. They sat in silence. The soldiers were advancing, and if they didn't get moving soon, they would be caught.

"What are we doing?" Ned snarled. "Are there oars? We need to get moving."

"Where are those two?" Norbert threw his paws up. "We told them we'd be right back."

Tino rolled his eyes and headed to the front of the boat. "Vesna! Luka!" He stared off into the horizon, looking for something.

"They do this to us all the time," Norbert said to Pierre. "Every time we ask them for help, they can't just help. They have to make a show of it. And now they're going to get us killed."

Ned growled. "Why aren't we moving?"

The stillness of the water broke. Two sea otters emerged side by side, wearing nothing over their fur. They had white fur faces with nearly identical markings. The only difference between them was the scars marring the body and nose of Luka.

Norbert uncrossed his arms. "About bloody time."

A small pod of dolphins swam in the shallow waters nearby.

"We're in a bit of a hurry, mates." Pierre motioned to the road.

Vesna and Luka took the ends of the ropes Norbert and Tino had thrown into the water and gave them to the dolphins. All seven dolphins had ropes in their mouths and proceeded to pull the boat forward.

Luka emerged on the left side of the boat and Vesna on the right. They kept pace with the boat, which trolled toward the larger part of the harbor.

Luka and Vesna whistled. Gray dolphins appeared next to them. Ned stared in awe. It had been many years since the northern sea otters and the spear dolphins had hunted together.

Dolphin riders had become a thing of legend, stories for cubs and pups. Ned had assumed all the dolphin riders were dead.

Luka gently petted the dolphin's head. In unison, they dove down, and Luka reemerged riding on the dolphin's back. Ned felt an urge to clap but managed to keep his composure.

Luka shook his head to clear the water from his face. "We'll pick up some speed now. Shouldn't be much longer."

Luka and his dolphin disappeared beneath the ocean's surface. Ned looked over his shoulder. Two of the guards stood on the dock. They tossed their spears. Ned ducked as one sailed over them and the other stuck into the side of the boat, splintering the wood.

Pierre wiggled the spear free. He held it up. "Thank you! We needed a new one of these!"

The jaguars roared and cursed at them.

The boat jerked forward, and Ned nearly fell backward. It cut through the small, rippling waves created by their dolphin escort. Luka and Vesna periodically surfaced to breathe and to check on them.

Ned was still in disbelief. Never in his life did he think he'd see a dolphin rider. Now here he was, a bear with no titles, with a dolphin escort. He might be the first bear ever to have one. The guards launched arrows that splashed just short of hitting them.

Even though he didn't find anything funny, Ned couldn't stop laughing. The otters frowned at him. He didn't care, as he couldn't catch his breath from laughing. He couldn't believe dolphins were helping him escape the city.

# Chapter 8
# The Ironwill

The dolphins guided them by all the large vessels around Ned. Pelicans soared above and dove into the ocean to feed. Animals stopped what they were doing and stared at them. Tino pointed at one ship moored apart from the others.

Ned sucked in a breath, his chest tightening. The *Ironwill* was a galleon that served as a floating city for otters. Of the three masts, two towered into the sky, while the back one stretched half as high as the others. Various nets and ropes ran and connected the masts, the sails, and the deck. They were close enough now that he could see otters running up, down, and across the various ropes, getting ready to set sail.

Ned counted twenty gunports on the side they headed toward. The ship's gray-stained, wooden sides were as solid as a stone fortress. Patterned carvings accented windows on the stern. He hoped he'd get a room back there.

The rowboat pulled up alongside the *Ironwill*. Tino attached ropes lowered from the ship to the front and back of the boat. Ned looked straight up. The ship felt taller than almost any building in

Wexlin, but it still felt small to him. This would be his boundary for the unforeseen future.

The boat rose out of the water. Ned fell back and gasped, causing him to rock the boat further.

"Careful, Ned. My knots don't always hold." Tino laughed.

The rowboat was raised to the level of the deck and secured by some crew otters. The crew didn't pay them much attention as they hopped off the boat onto the whitewashed deck. Hardly anyone stopped to say hello. They all seemed to have a task that required their full attention.

"I'll show you to the mess hall and the kitchen." Tino adjusted the oversized pack on his back. "From there, Ivin can get you to your cabin."

Ned nodded, and they headed below deck. Various cries of corralled livestock erupted all around him. The pen of goats was overcrowded. The chicken coops smelled of several years' worth of poop from never being fully cleaned. However, the chicken coops were mild compared to the tubs of shellfish, which reeked of stale water and rotten fish. Ned gagged. The four large wooden tubs were half filled with water, but their occupants were piled up to the surface. A single hog tied to one of the posts made the most noise. His cries were a subtle reminder that Ned would have to do the slaughtering himself. He shuddered. He preferred fish, as slaughtering large mammals was not something he enjoyed.

Pierre and Norbert went their own way, and Ned followed Tino down a flight of stairs. The stairs weren't big enough for a bear's foot. The descent was so steep that Ned held on to the deck above to prevent himself from falling.

He followed Tino down into a dark room, which was lit only by a few open gunports, and through to the mess hall. One side had numerous tables and chairs nailed to the ground for the otters. The other side had two large tables. One was for creatures bigger than river otters—Ned, Jaja, Calico, and the other large animals. The door of the mess hall led to the galley. Ned smiled and pumped his fist a little when he saw a window.

There was a small brick hearth on the far wall and a small wood-burning stove near a set of stairs. Ned hardly expected a wood-burning stove. The brick hearth was an entirely different matter. It was built bigger than for otters but was still small enough that otters could use it. The flue led up into a pipe that ran out the back of the ship. The hearth, built on a brick foundation and enclosed in smooth cement, was a fine piece of craftsmanship.

Ivin scrubbed one of the counters with a brush, his simple green tunic hanging on him.

Ned's heart leapt as some weight lifted off his shoulders. Pierre had told him Ivin was already on the ship, but it was a relief to finally see him.

"We'll be leaving shortly. I've shown Ivin what I know. Got other duties to attend to now." Tino scurried off, his large pack swaying.

"I unloaded the gear and supplies," Ivin said.

"I'm so glad to see you. When you didn't come back, I expected the worst."

"They wouldn't let me risk going back to tell you. They placed me in a crate and smuggled me onto this ship that same night. They gave me a hammock in the galley with the rest of the crew."

"Do you want to sleep with the rest of the crew?"

"Yes. If you don't mind." Ivin's tongue darted in and out. "I want to try and fit in."

"Of course I don't mind."

Ivin smiled and adjusted the sleeve of his tunic.

"Any idea where I sleep?" Ned asked.

"Up here, bear," a familiar voice called from the stairwell.

Ned widened his eyes. "Up the stairs?"

There was some mumbling from above, then Calico Baco's face came into view. "Up here, Ned."

Ned grabbed his pack and headed up to a cabin. The sweet

smell of lavender eased his tension, and he stared up at the blue and green patterned sheets hanging from the ceiling. Calico lay reading in one of the three beds that made up the large but cramped quarters.

More colorful sheets covered the walls. Calico's area was highlighted with reds, while the third bed was awash in yellow and green. A large brown wool rug covered the deck.

"Boots off in the room." Calico didn't remove his gaze from his book. "I just had this place decorated for the three of us. No reason our living quarters have to be so dreary. This used to be the officers' mess hall. Seems all it took was a bear coming on board to get things properly made. The green area is yours." He gestured to the bed closest to Ned. "Closest to the kitchen."

Ned put his bags down. "Who's the third?"

Calico glanced up. "Jaja. Boots off."

Ned kicked off his boots. He patted his bed, then slowly eased onto it. It swayed under his weight.

"Special design by the beaver. Rocks like a crew hammock but big enough and strong enough to support us." Calico turned another page in his book.

Ned's whole body shook on the swaying bed until he found his balance. The mattress was like any normal stuffed mattress, firm enough to support his weight. He had expected to sleep on the floor on a layer of blankets, so this was a pleasant surprise.

"Should we be doing something?" Ned asked.

"Do whatever you feel you need to do."

Ned stretched. He still had time before he had to start preparing the midday meal. He sighed. He should get one last look at Wexlin before exploring his home further. Unsure of where to start, he stood and looked around.

"Through here and up the stairs. Turn around, walk to midship to the next set of stairs, and you'll be on the deck. Follow the sunlight." Calico pointed at where the yellow and red sheets met.

"Thank you."

There was a little bit of a bounce in Ned's step as he made his way through the sheets and up to the deck. Otters rushed around and at times bumped into him as they headed to whatever task they had to do before they set sail. The deck felt as crowded as the busy streets of Wexlin. Ned stood perfectly still, not knowing where he wouldn't be in some otter's way.

"Up here, Ned," Jaja said.

Jaja was dressed like he was about to attend a formal ball. His green coat had all the necessary frills that complemented his canary-yellow shirt and trousers. He stood by the large spoked wheel, with Captain Elick Mandrin standing on the platform above him.

"Come up here, Ned," Jaja said. "You can see the city one last time. Jaja will let you steer when we get out of the harbor."

"Jaja!" The captain gave him a stern look.

"Ah, calm yourself, Captain. It's good luck for a nautical novice to hold the helm," Jaja said as Ned made his way up the steep ladder. "That's why captains always let cubs hold the wheel when they're aboard."

"Never let a pup take the helm," the captain said.

"This sleepless bear will have to do instead." Jaja hugged Ned. "We're about to set sail to worlds you've only dreamed of. Take a final look at Wexlin. Remember why we're doing this. We're going to save that city."

Jaja guided Ned to the railing to get one last look at the city Ned had called home for half a year. Any thoughts of jumping off and swimming for the shore were squandered at seeing the city guard on the shoreline. Ned squinted. Lord Gallant had managed to reform his ranks, and he and his soldiers rowed boats out to the *Ironwill*.

"Captain," Jaja said. "Should we load the cannons?"

"There's no need for that." Mandrin collapsed his spyglass. "Weigh anchor!"

## Ned Bear

Jaja echoed his orders, and within moments, the *Ironwill* left Wexlin's harbor and headed for their first stop at Crocodile Island.

* * *

Ned's legs buckled as he stumbled to the railing. He had given up trying to do it on two legs and had resorted to crawling. His elbows dragged along the wooden planks, his fur getting stuck between the boards as they bowed under his weight. It took all his strength, but he reached the railing and deposited his lunch into the ocean...again.

His limbs ached as if weighed down by cannonballs, and his head spun as more bile shot up his throat. Everything he had eaten for the last two days he had returned to the sea. "Goran's bargain," the crew called it. Goran allowed all novice sailors safe passage as long as they fed his fish. This was his bargain with the mortal creatures.

Ned wiped his mouth with the back of his paw, adding to the crust already formed on his fur from the day's bargaining. He rolled his way back to the center of the deck, lay on his back, and stared past the sails to an overcast sky. He couldn't even get lucky with the weather.

He had done his best to perform his duties as a cook, but most of the time he felt too weak to stand. Luckily for Ned and the crew, Ivin was a natural in the galley. He had taken over all of Ned's duties. Tino, to the disapproval of the entire crew, was back in the kitchen, helping Ivin. By Ivin's own admission, the food wasn't as good as Mama's or Ned's but was easily better than Tino's. Nonetheless, Ned couldn't keep it down.

He couldn't wait to get off this ship. He was told Goran's bargain got easier every time you got on and off his ocean. He was afraid he wouldn't get back on the *Ironwill* at all. They would be at Crocodile Island by nightfall, and the otters had painted such a vivid picture of the island's beautiful white sand beaches.

Ned's stomach turned on him quickly, and he sat up to crawl to the railing. His heart thumped. His cheeks filled before he was ready, and he lunged forward to avoid a disaster. He catapulted everything that was left in his stomach into the ocean. To be sure, he bargained some stomach phlegm, then gasped for air as tears welled in his eyes. He threw his arms over the railing, collapsed, and waited for the next round of hurling to begin.

Jaja chuckled and locked the wheel into place to stand by Ned. "Soon we'll be on land, my dear friend." He patted Ned's shoulder. "You will be the first bear to walk among the crocodiles. The riches you will see, Ned. Jewels and diamonds in carts right on the street."

"Right on the street? Why?"

"Are you willing to risk your paw over some gems? Jaja isn't faster than a crocodile snap. Captain says we'll make port for two nights. A good meal. A good sleep. You'll feel better next time we're on board. Jaja promises."

"I don't think I'm cut out for a life at sea." Ned buried his head in his paws. "I can't even cook. Tino and Ivin have been doing it all for me. I'm just unnecessary deadweight."

"You'll be better soon. Besides, Tino has improved much with Ivin's help. The crew hasn't complained. Hopefully they manage to come up with another meal, though. You must have shown Ivin how to do only the one." Jaja smiled and returned to the wheel. "Hang in there. Jaja will have us there before nightfall."

Jaja held up a clouded crystal he called his sunstone. He squinted through it with one eye.

"Land ho!" the lookout shouted from the crow's nest.

"The tides are with us, Ned." Jaja grunted as he turned the wheel. "We'll be there very soon."

Ned was dizzy but was able to stand despite his bones feeling like jelly. A green dot nestled on the horizon. He squinted to see it until it grew larger. The single mountain became multiple sea cliffs as the *Ironwill* slowed its pace into the shadow of the island. The green sea cliffs were accented with red rocks that punctuated the narrow valleys.

Waterfalls cut through the rocks and flowed down the mountainside. Ned smiled. The waterfalls reminded him of home and swimming beneath them with his sister, Ruby. *A simpler time.* One valley had several small waterfalls that created water steps that led into the rainforest. Another looked like several white snakes crawling down through the red rocks.

Captain Mandrin emerged from his cabin. He remained on the top deck away from the rest of the crew, armed with his spyglass that he fidgeted with when he was not using it.

The *Ironwill* drifted around the sea cliffs on the southwest side of Crocodile Island while the sunset colored the sky orange.

"The *Ironwill* is infamously fast. She'll be even faster once we get her careened. Outrun or run down anything that floats," Jaja said, repeating the phrase the crew often chanted.

The smoother motion of the vessel at the slower pace didn't make Ned feel nearly as sick. The crew rolled up sails and performed other tasks for preparing to dock. Ned couldn't wait to get off the ship.

Tino promised he'd show Ivin and Ned around once they were ashore. Jaja told him since he was considered an officer on the *Ironwill*, Ned could be on the first boat ashore. This made Ned happy. The faster he could get ashore, the faster he could get into an inn and a warm bath.

Pierre patted his back and sat next to him. "I promise you, it won't be like this forever."

Ned stuck his tongue out and blew a raspberry at Pierre.

Pierre chuckled. "Just try and remember the inns are made for crocodiles. Large, warm pools in each room. I had four, um, friends stay over, and the bed was plenty big enough for five of us. Or was it six?" He rubbed his chin. "Wonder if they're all still there?" He fell silent for a moment. Then he laughed as he stood and patted Ned on the back again. "Some otters just really love the lute."

"Pierre!" Guidry called from the deck below. "We need your help with the anchor." He frowned at Ned.

Ned raised an eyebrow at Guidry, who quickly avoided his gaze. Ned tried not to think much of it. He was excited to learn more about the island's cuisine. The crew had described it as having its own unique flavor. The island's rolling inland hills allowed the bison ranching to flourish. Their bison steaks had even made their way to the mainland and were infamously tender. The harbor's market was large enough that Ned anticipated finding new spices to try. Hopefully he'd find an eager crocodile to teach him a new recipe or two.

"You can learn how to make meals?" Amina stood over Ned.

He squinted up at her. "I can."

"Will you learn how to cook 'old clothes'?"

Ned flinched back and squished his eyebrows together. "I could. I don't know how good it's going to taste. Can't imagine clothes are going to be easy to swallow."

Amina took a throaty, deep breath and rolled her eyes. "It's the name of the dish. Slow-cooked bison flanks with tomatoes, onions, peppers, and puma roots all served in a bowl. Like a stew. It's delicious, and I would like to have it again when we're out at sea."

Ned smiled. "I'll do my best to find the recipe."

Amina frowned and barked commands at crew members who were standing around.

Ned had been fortunate to have found so many kind strangers to share their cooking with him. Mama told him, "They were keeping your belly full and happy so your eyes wouldn't wander onto them."

Ned hated that she was likely right. Most creatures were concerned that a bear would eat them. He would never eat a civilized creature. Creatures blessed by the gods that could read, write, and stand upright would never make for a good meal. He preferred to eat the cleaner meat of the wild, untouched animals of the Land. Salmon was his favorite. He'd never grow tired of eating it. He preferred bison, deer, moose, and insects over anything that wore breeches.

Shouting and barking sounded from the quarterdeck as Jaja, Guidry, Amina, Kenson, and the captain argued. Ned had seen this before—a battle was in the near future.

"What is it?" he asked.

The officers glared at him.

"Sailor!" the captain said. "Now is not the time to disturb us. Find something to do."

Ned snorted and grunted. The hairs on the back of his neck rose. He was trying to help, and the captain yelled at him. He tightened his fist and clenched his jaw. He was going to say something.

Jaja whistled and motioned for Ned to calm down. This only made him want to hit Jaja first. He took a deep breath instead. The captain paced on the deck. He'd occasionally pause to look through his spyglass, then would continue pacing. Ned could see now that his question wasn't the reason the captain had yelled at him.

If they were in danger, the crew seemed oblivious to it. Everyone moved around with the excitement of visiting port. It wasn't until the *Ironwill* completely rounded the bend that cannon fire erupted. The crew went from laughing and joking to complete silence. They were supposed to be heading to the entrance of the island's southern harbor, but it had been blocked.

This was a major trade route, yet there were no other ships on the open ocean except for the *Ironwill*. Four ships blocked the southern harbor and unloaded volleys of cannon fire into the harbor and port city. They didn't seem to notice the *Ironwill* trolling in the shallow waters behind them.

"Your orders, Captain?" Jaja asked.

The captain said nothing. He only squinted through his spyglass.

"Captain?" Jaja asked again.

Mandrin slammed the spyglass shut, his eyes wide. "Jaguar Navy."

Ned's heart sank. Another battle had found him. He crossed his arms. *I knew I shouldn't have gotten on this ship. Would've been better off just fighting all of Wexlin myself.* He wasn't sure what was going to happen, but he was certain of one thing: he wasn't getting off the ship.

# Chapter 9
# The Siege of Crocodile Island

The crew sprang into action. They hoisted the sails in between the masts to get the *Ironwill* back to full speed. The four ships laying siege to the harbor had noticed the *Ironwill*, and one of the sloops was in pursuit. The vessels sent cannon fire their way, testing their range.

"Load the starboard cannons!" the captain shouted, his commands quickly echoed throughout the ship.

"What should I do?" Ned asked Jaja.

"Stay there!" the captain said. "If they board us, we're going to need your help. Stay out of sight for now."

Ned looked around for a weapon just in case. Nothing. Instead, he found a cleaning bucket with rags. He shredded the rags, preparing to wrap his paws. Wrapping them strengthened his claws, protected his paws when punching, and enabled him to grab swords away from attackers. He didn't want to hurt his fingers by punching another helmet. His paw was just starting to feel good again.

"We're sailing against the wind. We're not going to lose them," Jaja said.

"Slip through the channel."

"Captain, we'll take significant damage if we lose the wind."

"Then don't lose it." The captain turned his attention to the crew. "Ready all square sails, and brace yourselves for a turnaround!"

"Captain, Jaja must insist—"

The captain narrowed his eyes. "I must insist you concentrate, Jaja. Our lives are in your hands. Slip through the channel, and double back around the Floating Island to the harbor."

Jaja nodded. "Jaja likes this plan."

The captain barked more orders as the crew moved about in organized chaos. Cannon fire echoed behind the *Ironwill*. A few hundred yards from the mainland was the Floating Island. It was a tall green mountain about a half mile long with no shallow water around it.

The captain ventured to the stern. "They're closing fast!"

"Don't worry. Jaja will handle it."

Jaja struggled to keep the wind in their sails and the cannonballs off their deck. One moment he would strain to hold the wheel in one direction, and the next he'd use all his strength to turn it the opposite direction. Even in the face of death, Jaja had a big smile on his face. The *Ironwill* quietly zigzagged through the narrow channel. Only the repeated cannon fire behind them disrupted the sound of the ocean.

A loud bang and cries from a wounded otter sent the crew into fits of squeaks and squeals. A cannonball had skimmed their port side, breaking up a small portion of their railing. Ned couldn't see who had been hit. The crew surrounded whoever it was and took them below deck. Ned's stomach jumped up to his throat. He hoped it hadn't been one of his friends.

Cannonballs crashed into the side of the *Ironwill* and rained down on her decks. *Tino had better be right about the sides being as solid as steel.* A small fire erupted near the mainmast. Ned grabbed the barrel of water the sailors used to dump their pipe ash and tossed it at the mast. The barrel shattered, and black water extinguished the flames. A couple of unfortunate otters who were trying to put out the fire were now wet and covered in muddy ash. Both glared at him with bulging eyes, baring their teeth while wiping the ash from their faces.

"Nice going, Ned!" Jaja strained to turn the wheel. "We're almost clear, Captain!"

The *Ironwill* weaved through the channel, smoking and damaged and with the sloop in pursuit.

"Ned! I suggest you find something to hold on to." The captain tied a rope around his waist and secured it to the stern railing.

Ned looked around for a rope or something but found nothing. He'd just have to hold on to one of the rails.

"Sails, ready! Guns, stand by! Hold steady!" When the captain spoke to Jaja, his voice was calm and firm. "Are we ready?"

"On your orders, Captain."

The captain gripped the railing. "Steady! Now, Jaja!"

Jaja turned the wheel sharply, and the ship began to list. A wave engulfed Ned, drenching his fur, and he skidded to one side and crashed into the railing.

"Roll back, Ned!" the captain yelled.

The deck was steeper and wetter than Ned had anticipated. He panicked and lost his grip while trying to pull himself up. He slipped and slid back to the railing.

"Roll back!" the captain cried out again.

A rope appeared nearby, and Ned sprawled to get it. He grabbed it and pulled himself up. Jaja's laugh rang behind him.

The ship tipped back the other way, and Ned rolled to the port side. He held the rope and buried his claws into the deck. His stomach bounced, and he thought the ship was going to capsize.

"Sails!" the captain said.

The crew hoisted fourteen square sails. The *Ironwill* jerked forward, now going in the opposite direction, and Ned's claws pulled free from the deck. He tumbled backward only to be stopped abruptly by the stern cabin's wall.

"Third deck!" the captain screamed, his words repeated by various members of the crew. "Fire!"

The cannon fire rocked the *Ironwill* from its momentum forward. Eyes wide, Ned sat pinned up against the wall. His heart raced. He wasn't used to fighting an enemy he couldn't see.

"Any hits?" Jaja asked.

"One or two tapped her. May buy some time for them to regroup and pursue," the captain said. "Reload!"

The Floating Island was on the *Ironwill*'s starboard side and provided a small window of peace as they backtracked to the harbor. They picked up speed with the wind at their backs. The mood on deck had drastically changed from their first approach to the island. The crew's faces were solemn as everyone worked in silence. They had been caught unprepared and were being pursued by the royal navy of the south. The *Ironwill* cleared the Floating Island, where the three ships still peppered the harbor.

"Take us into range, Jaja." The captain narrowed his eyes and clenched his jaw. "Let's see if we can get lucky."

Jaja turned the wheel toward the three navy ships. The ships stopped firing at the mainland. The *Ironwill* would be in range before the navy could prepare a proper counterattack. The massive man o' war in the middle unloaded a few rounds of cannon fire that fell well short of its target. The *Ironwill* turned to show the ship her broadside.

"All guns ready!" Norbert shouted from below deck.

The captain held his sextant—an instrument Ned had learned was used to measure the horizon of the ocean—to his eye and lined up the mast with his paw. He dropped the sextant and winked at Ned. "Fire!"

Thunder roared from the gun deck as the *Ironwill* unloaded her twenty cannons. The cannonballs soared over the shallow waters toward their target. Ned thought his heart had stopped for what seemed like an eternity. The silence was broken by the sound of shattering wood, followed by cheers from the crew.

"Reload! Fire at will!" the captain said. "Get us out of here, Jaja!"

"Right away, Captain."

The cannons volleyed a couple rounds on two of the navy ships while they returned fire, which skimmed the *Ironwill*'s sides.

Ned's throat was so dry he had to swallow hard to talk. "What just happened?"

"Jaja believes we declared war on the jaguars and the jaguars declared war on the crocodiles. The jaguars appear to have moved their war from the west coast to the crocodiles. Seems the empire has expanded its war of exterminating the reptiles to here." He scratched his head, then his chin. "Doesn't make much sense but a bold strategy. How is your stomach?"

Ned thought about it for a moment. His stomach didn't hurt. It was like he was on land again.

"I feel good. Not sick at all."

Jaja laughed. "The sound of cannon fire will cure most ailments."

The *Ironwill* sailed west into the sunset. Ned struggled to calm his rapid breathing and racing heart. Hopefully the setting sun would hide their path from the jaguar royal navy.

* * *

Ned couldn't sleep that night. He didn't understand how anyone could, but like every night, half the crew went to sleep while Amina took charge. Most of the faces he didn't know, but they all greeted him. After all, he was the only bear on the ship.

He started his sleepless night in the galley. Making food comforted him. It also gave him a feeling of self-worth. For the first time since leaving Wexlin, he felt better. Occasionally, his stomach would leap when he felt the waves underneath his legs, but it didn't make him sick. The cannon fire really did cure his illness. Despite the danger the *Ironwill* had been in, Ned had selfishly wished they fired the cannons on the first day.

His fear was dusted into the flour as he spent the first part of the night kneading dough to make bread. While he rotated bread and dough in and out of the hearth, he prepared a cauldron for stew. He remembered many cold nights off on his own, throwing the single fish he'd caught into the large pot and adding ingredients to stretch its nourishment.

Other bears would starve if they couldn't catch enough fish every day. Not Ned. He learned early on how to use vegetables to satisfy his hunger. He diced celery, onions, and carrots and tossed them into the pot with some goat butter. He stirred and seasoned them with salt and pepper and a touch of fresh dill. He hung the pot over the open flames of the hearth and let his vegetables simmer. He diced some potatoes and added goat's milk to the now bubbling pot.

He pulled the remaining salted fish from a barrel. They were poorly cut for small fillets, which didn't matter to him. There was cod, haddock, and striper. He'd found some shrimp and scallops in a separate barrel he'd utilize as well. He tossed the shellfish into the pot and tore apart the salted fillets. He stirred the stew, but it looked too watery. He had forgotten the flour. He added flour, and the stew smelled of salty clams and cream.

Calico popped his head down from their room. "What are you cooking?"

"Stew. A fish one the otters will like."

"Good." Calico came down the stairs with his paws full of parchments and old leather-bound books. "We'll all need a good meal before the battle. We can't outrun the navy forever." He paused and glanced at the empty barrels that previously housed the salted meat. "You may want to use less rations. More roots, less fish."

"Wanted to make something good."

Calico frowned before holding up the parchments. "While you were sick, I took the liberty of sorting and reading through these. I suspect you are fully unaware of their contents or perhaps are all too trusting?"

"You went through my things?" Ned put down the knife he held. His nostrils flared, and his muscles and veins strained against his skin.

"I assure you, every single piece of parchment has been returned to you. I merely read what I could and organized it. My apologies if I offended you. I've read almost every book this ship and Wexlin have to offer, and my curiosity seems to have killed my manners."

Ned took a deep breath, forcing himself to relax. "What did you find?"

"What are *Bojana's Articles of War?*" Calico held it up. "I couldn't read the pages. They're written in bear script. Is it about the war and her curse?"

"No." Ned took back his book. "Long before the gods' war, Bojana wrote this. She was the goddess of peace. She knew she could never stop wars, so she provided these articles as a guideline. Sort of rules of engagement and ways to seek peace before combat. After the Great Purge of the old gods, bears rewrote the articles in bear as a way to keep the book. It's the only book bears are allowed to read. Don't want us filling our heads with ideas not related to war."

Ned ran his paw pad over the leather cover. He handed it back to Calico before a wave of bad memories overtook him.

"Nothing about her curse?"

"No, that came much later. What are those parchments?"

"Did you know these were written by Labarre?"

Ned stepped over to look at what Calico had found. He couldn't believe it. Was he really traveling with parchments written by Labarre's own paw?

"I found this sketch of a map of the known world, much like the one the captain gave you. This appears to be an earlier draft. He marked on each mass of land where he had landed. Then he scribbled on the bottom here, 'My path will show you where.'"

"Interesting."

"That is hardly the interesting part." Calico spread out another parchment. "Several of these parchments state we're heading in the wrong direction." He tapped a small island north of the Island of Winter. Written on the bottom was "A turtle's back."

Calico placed a paw-drawn map over the larger one. This was of a single island with an X in the middle of what appeared to be a mountain.

"What island is this?" Ned asked.

"I believe it's Tortue, but it's also not in the right spot on any of these maps. Look here." He unrolled a parchment with a sketch of a square churchlike building. "'Bring a sleepless bear to my final resting place.' You see, according to this, we're going to the wrong island. There are directions written in these journals on how to solve a magic door and where his ship is. We should be going to Tortue before we go to Goran's ice island."

"His ship? The *Pelican* was lost at sea with Labarre. What are we going to tell the captain?"

"That I was right about Maydia and Bojana's barbute and this note from Labarre confirms it." Calico handed Ned the goatskin scroll. "Labarre believes the barbute is with the treasure, and if the barbute is retrieved by a bear, the curse will be over."

"Which would bring all the gods and magic back." Ned read it to confirm it for himself.

Calico looked through the pile. "Would that be a good thing?"

"I'm not sure." Ned stared through the words on the scroll. Would bringing back the gods be a good thing? Was he the bear to make that decision? Was the captain making that decision for him? Or was all of this really just a fool's quest like Mama said? So many questions soared through his head. Before he answered one question, a new one emerged. But there was only one he wrestled with: Would bringing back magic and the gods be a good thing?

"Ned, are you listening to me? This is why the *Dirty Whisker* hunts the oceans. Maydia killed my father and took that panda. Why hasn't he broken the curse yet?" Calico frowned. "Is Maydia capturing the bears to prevent the curse from breaking? We're missing something." He flipped through the parchments.

The galley door swung open.

"The captain needs to see you immediately, Calico," Kenson said.

Calico folded up the parchments and tucked them under his arm. "I'm busy. The captain can come see me if it's important enough. You can tell him I'll be ready to fight whenever the navy is about to board us."

"We're not being chased by the navy anymore."

"All is well, then."

"We're being pursued by the *Dirty Whisker*."

Calico froze. He stared at Kenson. "Well, I would say he's right on cue. Are you sure?"

Kenson nodded. "I saw the green sails myself."

"Perhaps I'll take a walk on the deck to go see the captain."

Calico handed Ned the parchments and left faster than Ned had ever seen him move.

"You too, Ned. Clean up, and the captain will speak with you after Calico."

"Do you have family on the island?" Ned suspected Kenson was from Crocodile Island.

"A wife. Our place is a couple days' ride from the harbor. She should have been clear of the attack. Our hatchlings are all grown. Some I have never met, as our children leave the nest when they're very young. Still, I worry for their safety." He cleared his throat. "There is no time for that now." He exited the galley, his tail knocking over a bucket on the way out.

Ned looked around the empty galley. Unsure of what to do, he cleaned up and stared at the glowing coals under his stew. *Maydia is real? And he's chasing us? Does he want to capture me or kill me? Can we really fight them off?* His body heated, and his head was swimming. So much had just happened that the idea of leaving the galley seemed impossible to him. Maybe if he stayed here, he wouldn't have to face what was coming next.

He closed his eyes and took a deep breath. Whatever Maydia wanted with him, he was about to find out.

# Chapter 10
# The Dirty Whisker

The *Dirty Whisker* was a jaguar warship with three large masts that each hoisted four green sails. Its black hull was highlighted by gold rails, while a carving of a jaguar with an extended sword graced the stern. It was nearly two hundred feet long with well over a hundred guns spread across the bow, stern, and three gun decks. It had always been feared and patrolled the southern waters for the jaguar emperor, and when it was said to be cursed, it had become even more of a legend. It was a horror story sailors told to keep other sailors in line, and now that ghost story was tethered to the *Ironwill*.

Tino, Pierre, and Norbert took Ned into the captain's quarters. They were to remain hidden until told otherwise. "Under no circumstances are you to leave the captain's quarters" was repeated to them by every officer on the ship.

"Only attack if all is lost. I will call for you when I need you. I don't wish to give Maydia what he wants." It was the last thing the captain said to Ned before closing the door to his cabin.

Legends said that Maydia and his crew were unable to walk on land. So Jaja and Amina emptied barrels of dirt at the doorway to further protect Ned from Maydia.

The captain insisted that in order to help sell the illusion they were not pirates, Ivin and the others needed to look like they were prisoners in case Maydia searched the lower decks. Pirates took slaves but rarely took prisoners. Even though Ivin and the others were armed and given a key, Ned didn't like being unable to watch over him.

"They probably don't want Maydia laying a trap." Pierre spun his pistols. "That jaguar has been hunting bears for over a hundred years."

Ned huffed and snorted. He narrowed his eyes and returned to looking out the portholes that overlooked the deck with Tino. Norbert went through the captain's stuff.

After the grand warship had chased them down, a series of flags were raised between the two vessels. They anchored side by side in a small island cove. The water was still, which Ned was thankful for. The captain's quarters were stale, hot, and humid, and even opening the windows did little to cool the room. Ned's panting grew heavy and rapid as he tried to cool himself.

Pierre folded some clothes. "You're going to have to find a way to be quieter with that, Ned."

"What are you doing?" Tino asked. "Are you going through his things?"

"No. I'm organizing them. I don't want him coming back here and thinking we messed it up." Pierre closed a storage trunk.

Pierre found something else to clean, and Norbert was now going through the cabin, commenting on everything he found. Tino and Ned remained fixated on the events taking place on deck.

Several planks of wood spanned the two ships, forming a temporary bridge. On the *Ironwill*, Captain Mandrin sat at attention in front of a cloth-covered barrel, which he had set up on the quarterdeck in front of his cabin. He was flanked by Natty Nimbles, Jaja, Amina, Kenson, and Guidry, all dressed in formal garments. The rest of the *Ironwill*'s crew lined up and stood at attention.

A door opened on the *Dirty Whisker* from the middeck, and two jaguar soldiers emerged. They were armed with large square shields painted blue and highlighted with an orange stripe. They wore light hide armor, their spotted yellow fur only visible on their forearms and face. Their armor looked new, but the style and fit were dated.

The two soldiers crossed the bridge to the *Ironwill*'s deck and stood at attention. A tall jaguar strutted across the boards like he owned the sea he walked over. Roberto Maydia. He wore no armor but had donned a more elegant version of the dated blue-and-orange uniform. Following Maydia across the bridge were two ocelots and two more jaguar soldiers.

Captain Mandrin shifted in his chair and turned to whisper something to Jaja. Jaja nodded and exchanged a glance with Amina, who frowned. The soldiers stood back-to-back in the center of the deck, locking their shields in place and preventing the *Ironwill*'s crew from advancing on the stairs. Maydia and the two ocelots made their way up the quarterdeck. They were a mere ten feet from Ned now, separated only by a cabin wall. Maydia was all smiles when the captain motioned for him to sit.

He took a seat and casually leaned back and crossed his legs. Captain Mandrin sat stiffly opposite him. A breeze fluttered the cloth on the barrel, and the empty tankards tipped over.

Ned wiped his breath off the porthole glass, and Pierre cracked the door so they could hear better.

"Sir, I believe we agreed to host you and four others. You have brought six. I must protest," the captain said.

Maydia gave a half smile. "Captain, these ocelots are my scribes. I must have them near me at all times. You'll have to forgive me, as I'm very forgetful. Comes with age, I fear. I must insist on your allowing my four guards for my protection from your soldiers and your bear."

There was a long silence as Maydia loomed over Mandrin.

Captain Mandrin poured them both some wine. "What can I do for you?"

Maydia snickered, threw back his head, and swallowed his cup of wine. "My name is Captain Roberto Maydia. I am here for one thing and one thing only. Give me the bear, and you and the rest of your crew can be on your way."

"Sir, I haven't the slightest idea what you're talking about." Mandrin sipped from his cup.

Maydia spun his empty cup around like a cub's toy before placing it back on the cloth. "The barrels of dirt you have poured in front of your quarters and the entrance to your cargo hold lead me to believe you know who I am and you are hiding something from me. And if you know who I am, you know I'm only interested in one thing. So I'll ask you again politely. Where is the bear?"

"Before I answer, may I be permitted to ask you a question?" The captain took another sip.

"Apart from the question you just asked, by all means. Proceed, Captain."

"What in the name of the gods are you intending to do with a bear?"

Maydia studied him, then glanced at his officers. He adjusted his uniform, sliding his paws over his buttons. "Treasure hunting is a bold, risky, and foolish endeavor. Something only ignorant cubs seek. My ship, my crew, and I did our duty to our emperor. He challenged those more powerful than him, and we paid the price. He's cold and in the ground, and here we are, cursed to circle these waters until we undo his wrong. A bear will get me to Goran, and it's Goran whom I need to have words with. And hear my warning, otter. The treasure you seek is cursed. Leave it be, and give me the bear."

"You didn't answer my question." Mandrin adjusted his tail on the chair. "After all these years, you haven't gotten a bear? I don't believe that. What are you doing with them?"

Maydia grinned and leaned back. "The same thing you intend to do. Take them to the treasure, retrieve the barbute, bring back the magic, and reverse this curse so my ship and crew can finally rest. There are complications once the bear gets to the island. None of them have ever returned."

The captain eyed his cup before taking a long, deliberate sip. "And if I don't have a bear?"

"Come, Captain, don't force me to have my crew board your ship to question your entire crew with a sword. I know he's here. I can smell him. My ship seeks him and knows when one is on the water."

"Perhaps a third proposition, a Detos duel for my ship's safe passage and the bear." Mandrin grinned.

Maydia smirked and looked at the *Ironwill*'s officers. "You don't have a suitable warrior to challenge my champion. Spare your crew the loss."

"I'll be your kitty cat." Calico's voiced echoed from the deck below the captain's quarters.

He cleared his throat, and the jaguars opened their shields to let him emerge onto the quarterdeck. Calico's armor was plated red-and-gold polished steel over butted mail. His shoulders and thighs were protected with plates, while the red-and-gold fabric covered down to his ankles.

He wore no helmet and carried no shield. Instead, his arm was covered in overlapping plates that ran from his shoulder down to his wrist. He was an entire head taller than the jaguars, and he made sure Maydia knew it as he stalked around him.

"Such a lovely uniform, Captain. The stitchwork is very elegant and tight." Calico pushed away a spear a soldier had pointed at him. "I've waited nearly my entire life to find you again, Maydia. You're far frailer than I remember. You boarded my father's ship and slaughtered him. You didn't see the cub with his mother hiding in the captain's quarters as you ransacked the deck. I haven't forgotten you. And you will meet the same fate as my father. You die here today."

"We're going to be fine." Tino's gaze remained fixated on the porthole. "Calico wins duels all the time. He was a champion fighter."

Stiff as a boulder, Ned rubbed his shoulder. He didn't like any of this. *I should be the one fighting. It's me they're after. I can beat one jaguar with ease. They should let me fight.*

"How often do you do these duels?" Ned asked.

"Pirate code," Tino said. "Raise the black flag. We want your stuff, but there is no sense in killing and blowing up each other's ships for it. Sometimes a ship wants an honest fight to defend itself. So we have a duel. Named after the god of law and justice."

Ned got the impression they did these duels often.

Armed with two swords, Calico stood across from the jaguar champion, who was announced as Emeric Larios. Emeric had foregone his spear in favor of a small forearm shield and a club. The club looked like an oar with a short handle, its sides embedded with multiple prismatic black blades that looked like teeth. This was a traditional weapon in the south, but this was the first time Ned had seen a macuahuitl. Emeric swung the macuahuitl, its black blades glistening in the afternoon sunlight. Calico stood in the center of the bridge and yawned. In his paws were the moon steel sword that gradually curved up to the tip and a parrying dagger made of dull silver. Calico clashed his dagger to the moon steel sword and motioned for Emeric to start.

Emeric held his club over his head and roared to his ship. They responded in kind. He swung the club at Calico. Calico sidestepped and ducked. Emeric snarled and swung down on him. Calico stepped back, letting the club slam into the bridge, some of its blades shattering on contact. He struck Emeric's club, spun forward, and sliced with his dagger. Emeric pushed him away with his shield, roared, and unleashed a whirlwind of attacks. Calico dodged or parried them away. He had remained untouched.

A pistol fired. Calico flinched. He looked down at the plated armor on his arm, then shouted curses at someone on the *Dirty Whisker*.

"Foul play!" Mandrin stood and glared at Maydia. "I demand your champion forfeit the fight."

Maydia waved him off. "Your cat seems fine. Let them finish."

"Maydia, I demand your champion forfeit." Mandrin growled. "Your side shot at my champion. They interfered. By the laws of Detos and the other gods—"

Maydia stabbed his dagger into the barrel. "There are no gods." He placed a pistol next to his dagger, pointing it at Mandrin. "Let them finish the fight."

The duel never stopped. Calico twirled and swung what Ned thought were weak attacks on Emeric, who easily blocked all of them. *Calico is toying with him.* After a whirlwind of strikes, Calico kicked Emeric in the chest, which knocked him off his feet. He allowed Emeric to stand back up. Emeric gasped for air as his shield dragged on the planks and the macuahuitl hung by his side.

Emeric roared and swung down on Calico, trying to end the fight. Calico stepped back and allowed the macuahuitl's blades to shatter further into the planks. He sliced at Emeric's paw, and his weapon fell. The crew on the *Ironwill* erupted in cheers.

Calico said something to Emeric that Ned couldn't hear. Emeric shook his head, and Calico nodded before he impaled Emeric with his dagger and sliced him with his moon steel sword. Emeric fell into the sea. It was over.

The captain turned to a stunned Maydia. "We learned moon steel is stronger than any type of magic. Would you like me to escort you to your ship now?"

Maydia leapt to his feet. He glanced at his soldiers, who all shared looks of despair. He flashed a signal to his ship. A musket fired. Calico flinched, blinking rapidly. He touched his belly, then glanced at the blood coating his paw. He gasped before stumbling backward off the bridge and splashing into the sea.

Ned's heart stopped, his paws frozen to the floor. *Not Calico.* The four warriors on the deck of the *Ironwill* spread out and separated the *Ironwill*'s crew with their shields and spears. Four jaguars and six ocelots swung from the *Dirty Whisker* and landed on the quarterdeck to protect Maydia. The otters barked and returned pistol fire. Their bullets dinged off the large shields. They were easy prey on the exposed deck. Two ocelots took hold of Captain Mandrin.

Ned didn't want to fight, but they needed him now. He remembered his orders from the captain that they were not to leave his cabin until an officer came to get them. They all could be dead long before that. Ned glanced around for some sort of signal from one of the officers. Nothing.

"What do we do?" Ned whispered to Tino.

Tino had tears in his eyes, and his bottom lip wouldn't stop quivering. "I...I don't know. We were ordered to stay here."

"I've been courteous with you to a fault, otter." Maydia towered over the captain. "All I want is the bear. If you won't give him to me, I'll take him from you. Surrender him, or I'll see that your hull removes all your fur."

The ocelots tied up the captain and pulled him off the deck by his wrists. His ankles were restrained and attached to a rope coming out of the water.

"Is this what you want?" Maydia growled at a suspended Mandrin. "All I want is the bear. You could've had the treasure. Now all I offer is your life for the bear."

"What are you doing with them?" Mandrin asked.

Maydia yanked at the rope tied to his feet, and Mandrin screamed.

"This isn't your first bear, so why is there still a curse?"

Maydia's grin turned into a laugh. "I'm doing you a favor, otter. You are far too ignorant for the trials ahead. You would've led your crew to their doom." He handed the rope to two ocelots. "Go ahead and dunk him, and see if his officers are more willing to talk."

Fear consumed Tino's gaze. "They're going to keelhaul him."

"What's that?"

Tino gulped. "They're going to drag him along the bottom of the ship. Shredding him alive."

Ned's fur stood on end, and a fire burned in his belly. His breathing rapid, his paws tightened as he extended his claws. He looked at the officers on deck for some sort of sign for him to help. They remained helpless, their backs up against a wall, spears pointed at their throats.

"Ned!" Norbert stood by the doorway. He had strapped as many pistols as he could to his torso and held a white sword. "If you want to do something, now would be the time."

*This is it. All is about to be lost.*

Ned dashed to the door and crashed through it with all his force. He snorted and rose onto two legs. He roared as loudly as he could. Spit flew off his fangs as he raised his nose to the sky. He extended his arms and flashed his claws. He slammed back down onto four legs, ending his roar and shaking the ship.

Everyone froze, their wide eyes on Ned. He had warned them he was going to engage in combat. All those who heard him roar were given a chance to submit or flee. They did nothing.

Maydia reached for his sword. "There he is."

Ned growled and sprang into action. He surged toward the ocelots holding his captain up. The ocelots let go of the rope, and the captain thudded onto the deck. Ned grabbed the nearest jaguar and tossed him overboard like he was discarding seaweed after a swim. A swat with his left followed by a smack with his right sent a pair of bold, charging ocelots into the sea. Ned lunged at the two remaining jaguars on the quarterdeck.

They tossed a net over him. *Always a net.* Ned punched through the net, knocking a jaguar off his feet. The second jaguar stabbed at him, and Ned swung the net, which tangled the jaguar in the twine with him. Ned grabbed him by the throat, held him to his face, and roared. The jaguar scratched Ned's snout. Ned growled and slammed him into the deck before kicking him overboard. He ripped off the net and looked for another enemy.

Pistol fire thundered. Pain sliced into Ned's back. He touched the spot. No blood, but he felt the lump of a flesh wound. The bullet had hardly made its way through his fur. He turned to see Maydia holding a pistol.

"In the back?" Ned grabbed a sword off the deck.

The sword felt like a twig in his paw and was far too small for him to use offensively. He tossed it into his left paw for parrying attacks, leaving his right free for offense.

Maydia stuck his pistol in his belt and drew a second black sword. He twirled the blades. "Leave this ship with me, bear. I promise you the same riches they have. I need you strong." He banged his swords together. "A wounded bear won't survive the journey."

*A wounded bear? This tiny cat thinks he can beat me?* Ned roared at Maydia.

"So be it."

Maydia charged at Ned with his twin blades overhead. He brought the swords down on Ned. Ned used his sword to parry them away. The handle vibrated and stung his paw pad. Maydia spun and jumped, his blades slicing down. Ned was able to block one, but his sword was far too small, and Maydia's blade ran down the top of Ned's forearm.

Ned growled in pain as the blood oozed into his fur. His arm throbbed, now too weak to hold his sword. He roared again and then snarled directly at his wound, hoping that would heal it or at least stop it from hurting.

"I told you." Maydia lowered his swords. "Come with me. Let us stop this madness."

A pounding thudded in Ned's ears as his body started to shake. He would never give Maydia what he wanted. He tackled Maydia, sending his swords flying, and slammed him into the deck. He swung his leg over to press his weight on Maydia's chest. Ned could fully sit down and crush him at any time. Maydia hissed and snarled. Ned held a claw to his throat to stop him from squirming.

Ned glanced around. The crew had quickly retaken the *Ironwill*. Blood dripped from his fur, pooling on the planks and staining them crimson. His arm burned and throbbed. He winced as he tried to move it.

Scattered musket fire echoed from the *Dirty Whisker* with returned pistol fire from the *Ironwill*. They had not stopped attacking.

Ned snarled at Maydia. "Call your cats off!"

"I...can't with you...sitting on me."

Another round of musket fire rained down on the quarterdeck. The wood splintered around Ned. He got off and pulled Maydia up by the neck scruff.

"Call them off!"

Maydia waved his paws at his ship. "Cease fire! Cease fire!"

The musket fire stopped, and Maydia eyed Ned. "What will you do now, bear? Put me in chains and expect my ship to sail away? You think these rodents are your friends? You're bait to them. Come with me. End this curse for me and my crew. You can have the biggest cut of the treasure."

Someone wailed behind Ned. The otters' cries tore a hole in his heart. Tino and Norbert crouched next to Pierre, who lay on his back in a puddle of blood.

"Get up, Pierre," Tino said through tears.

Norbert tried to pull Pierre up off the deck. Pierre was awake but too weak to aid or resist.

"Come on, mate," Norbert said. "This ain't so bad. Come on." He tried to pick him up again.

Fire burned in Ned's chest, and he tightened his grip on Maydia's throat.

Jaja's large hand touched his shoulder. "Give him to Jaja. Jaja will take care of him."

Ned punched Jaja's hand away with his snout, not wanting to

move his hurt arm. Maydia clawed and hissed at him with little success. Ned walked up the ladder to the top deck, a sharp pain shooting down his arm with each rung he grabbed. Rather than show pain, he clenched his jaw and ignored his left arm, now drenched in his blood. He managed to raise Maydia high enough for his face to meet every single rung on the ladder as they slowly ascended. The *Ironwill* bobbed in the water in the eerie silence. He lifted Maydia up as high as he could before slamming him back down into the wooden planks.

Maydia groaned in pain before trying to scramble away. Ned pounced on him.

"You'll kill me in cold blood?" Maydia asked.

"You killed my friends."

"How will you do it? I'm cursed to sail these seas. I tried swallowing a bullet. I spit it back up and haven't gotten the taste of gunpowder off my tongue. I don't fear death. I welcome it."

"Leave us alone. My final warning to you, cat."

Ned grabbed him by the back of the neck and easily held him over his head with one paw. Once Ned was certain all eyes were on him, he roared loud enough for all the gods to hear.

When he finished, unusual ripples moved in the sea behind the *Dirty Whisker*—the same ones he had seen only once before. Luka, Vesna, and their dolphins emerged, and the red foxes, Big and Lil Eli, jumped from the back of the *Dirty Whisker* and swam toward the pod of dolphins.

Luka, Vesna, and the dolphins had been waiting with the foxes in the water the whole time. *They could have saved the captain.*

"Clever," Maydia said.

An explosion from the *Dirty Whisker* rocked the *Ironwill* and knocked Ned off his feet. Maydia slammed into the deck with a groan, then rolled away from Ned. The heat from the fire made Ned fear his face had been set ablaze.

The *Dirty Whisker* was engulfed in flames. The cats jumped overboard and splashed about, looking for something that floated.

Maydia leapt over the railing and into the sea. Ned growled. The next time he saw Maydia, he would make him pay for killing Calico and possibly Pierre. Pain spiked into his chest at the thought of losing Pierre. He swallowed hard as the *Ironwill* pulled anchor and hoisted the sails. All of this for some treasure. Was any of this worth it? Or would they all end up dead long before they reached it?

# Chapter 11
# The Storm

Where Ned had made stew the night before had been transformed into a makeshift hospital. The tables were now surgical stands for the one otter with medical experience, Felix Boucher. Boucher had dark-brown fur, nearly black, with patches of reddish brown that contrasted horribly with the rest, giving his face a twisted look. His white apron was stained with blood, but he did his best to wipe his paws clean.

Felix had been far too busy, so Ned dressed his own wound. He had done it many times before, although never one this big and deep. He licked the blood off his fur in order to see the gash better.

Felix handed him a bottle of alcohol. "Don't growl too loud and wake the others."

Ned snorted and took the bottle. He hated this part. He dumped the alcohol over the wound, and it burned. All he could do was snarl as the alcohol ran down the slice like a river in a valley. His paw shook as the last bit finally dropped from the bottle.

"Was it enough?" Felix nodded to the empty bottle.

"I sure hope so." Ned grimaced, looking over the slash. "I don't want to do that again."

"You gonna let me sew you up? Or you gonna insist on doing that yourself too?"

"You've got others to attend to. I've cleaned my own wounds before. But could you bring me that large jar of honey?"

Felix raised an eyebrow. "Hardly a time for a snack, Ned." He handed him the jar and some bandages.

Ned gave a small chuckle and then winced. "Old bear secret, my friend. Honey is delicious, but it's a snack with power." He slathered the wound with a thick coat of honey. He clenched his jaw, trying not to roar from the pain. "The honey numbs and heals better than any creation in a bottle."

"If you insist." Felix's whiskers twitched as he went to attend another patient.

Ned closed his eyes to try to slow his heavy breathing. He wanted to wait for the pain to die down a little before he started stitching. When it was time, he stitched up the cut with relative ease and only some pain. The alcohol had been the most painful part. He smeared another layer of honey over the wound before wrapping it in a fresh bandage. He was ready to help Felix again.

The *Ironwill* had lost Calico Baco and five otters during the parley with Roberto Maydia. When Felix told him so, Ned wrapped the dead otters in seaweed and canvas from a torn sail. That left three otters clinging to life in the ship's galley. Selfishly, Ned only thought of Pierre. He hadn't bothered to learn the names of the lifeless, wrapped bodies he had carried up to the deck to be buried at sea. Now he wished he could go back and learn everything possible about them.

When Ned returned, Norbert and Tino were still sitting outside the door, waiting for news. Asleep, they leaned against each other. Ned startled them awake. They looked up at him with wondering eyes. Ned pushed the door open, which caused it to slam into one of the tables.

"Damn!" Felix said before seeing it was Ned. "Oh, sorry. Thought you were one of them sleeping outside. Thank you for taking the fallen up for me."

Ned nodded and checked on Pierre. The bullet had hit him in the belly and had gone out the back. Felix checked to make sure there were no bullet fragments and confirmed it had gone clear through. Now they could only wait. If they had been on land, Ned could have found a shaman with more experience and resources than Felix. But right now, he was all they had.

Felix patted Ned's back. "Let him be judged by the Great Spirit now."

Ned snorted at his sympathy. The mere mention of the Great Spirit or the gods at a time like this seemed cubbish. It's what creatures said when they were out of answers. A shaman could save his friend. He should've saved his friend.

"May the Great Spirit allow him to stay with us." The words felt awkward coming out of Ned's mouth. He knew the gods were gone, banished because of Bojana's curse. The gods had stopped watching over these lands long ago.

"Can Norbert and Tino come in and visit?" Ned asked in a tone that made it clear he wasn't really asking.

"As long as they don't make a bunch of noise." Felix walked away.

"Ned," Pierre said weakly.

Ned's heart leapt. But his joy quickly washed away at the loss of life in Pierre's face. His tongue lodged in his throat. "Yes?"

"We're mates, right?"

"Yes."

Pierre sighed. "Good. I...I was never sure if ya thought of us as mates."

He had known Pierre for less than a month, and yet he, Ivin, Tino, and Norbert were his closest friends.

"You're the best fisher I've ever seen," Ned choked out.

Pierre smiled. "You bears are buffalo chips unless the fish

jumps into your mouth."

They chuckled. Pierre's chuckle turned into a cough, and he winced in pain. When he regained his strength and composure, he looked at Ned with a steady stare.

Ned wished he could think of more to say. He wanted to tell Pierre that everything was going to be all right, but he knew he couldn't. He thought about promising him revenge, but Pierre wouldn't want to hear that. If there was only a way to fix this. Maybe if he could get him to a shaman soon, there would still be time. Ned's stomach soured. His chest felt like a buffalo was sitting on it as he did his best to fight back tears, knowing all he could do was sit there and listen to Pierre.

"Berty and Tino... Will you watch over them for me? They're the only family I have, and they'll be lost."

The tear Ned had been forcing back fell out. "Of course I will."

Pierre patted Ned's paw. "Don't let Tino play my lute. He doesn't trim his claws and scratches up the finish."

Ned laughed. Here even in his final hours, Pierre was trying to comfort him.

"May I ask you one final favor?" Pierre's voice had grown frailer.

"Anything."

"Don't let them bury me at sea. I don't want to be eaten by sharks and crabs. Please."

"Don't think that way. You're going to walk out of here in a couple of days."

Pierre gave him a half-hearted smile. "Ned, there is something you should know. Calico had me translate Labarre's writings, the ones the old otter gave you."

"I don't care about that."

"No, listen." Pierre grabbed Ned's paw, and his eyes darted around the room like he was making sure no one else was listening. "There is more to Goran's gold. The barbute is magical. The magic is locked in the metal."

"I know. That's why we're going to get it. That's why Maydia wants it."

"That's why everyone has been trying to take a bear there." Pierre choked on a cough. "In success all shall be blessed. The barbute breaks Bojana's curse."

"A bear needs to put on Bojana's barbute to bring back the magic to undo Bojana's curse?"

"Yes. That's why Maydia wants you. But Labarre wrote a bear has to put Bojana's barbute on. Don't let them put the helmet on you. Labarre also wrote he watched bears being dragged before Goran only to put the helmet on and die. It didn't lift the curse. It only killed the bears. I read it twice to be sure. Don't put the barbute on. It's a trick." Pierre squeezed his paw and then broke out into a coughing fit.

The galley door swung open and slammed against the table. Felix cursed at the door and then at those who had come in. Tino and Norbert tiptoed in, their tricorn hats held in front of them. They both nervously twisted the brims.

"The captain has sent for you, Ned," Tino said.

Both of them hardly looked at him, their eyes fixed on their friend.

"In a moment." Ned needed to know more about what Pierre had read.

"It's not up to me, mate." Norbert took a seat by Pierre. "The fellows outside are waiting for you."

Ned sighed and stood. "See you soon, my friend."

He squeezed Pierre's paw before heading out of the galley to give the three otters some time to talk. Big and Lil Eli and Luka and Vesna greeted him.

"Takes the four of you to come get me?"

"Aye." Luka's deep voice bellowed in the narrow hallway. "Captain is in a fit. He couldn't decide who to send. When he waved his paw in our direction, we took it as an excuse to leave."

They didn't say anything further. They walked in silence. Only the creaking of the wooden planks interrupted the rhythmic rolling of the ocean waves. When they reached the quarterdeck, Natty Nimbles was measuring and shaking his head at the splintered wood where the door had once been. He scratched his head, measured, and shook his head again. As Ned lumbered over to him, the others headed below deck.

Natty rubbed the back of his neck, then bared his teeth at Ned. "I'm going to have to replace the entire front wall when we dock." He waved at the damage.

Ned resisted the urge to roll his eyes. "Sorry."

"Send that bear in!" Guidry shouted from the captain's quarters.

Ned expected a hero's welcome. Instead, he was greeted with glaring eyes and clenched jaws.

"Sit and don't say a word." Guidry pointed to the empty chair across from Jaja and Amina.

Guidry paced the quarters and muttered to himself. The captain's quarters had changed since Ned was told to hide inside. The beds had been moved out of sight along with any other personal items that had been left out. Now a single table with two lanterns dominated the interior of the cabin. The light from the lanterns flickered on the emotionless faces of Jaja and Amina.

Ned wished someone would say something. This was not the greeting he had expected. He had expected drinks, cheers, and some merriment. Not the stony, solemn glare the officers had locked onto him. Behind him, an approaching otter's pace quickened. He didn't need to turn around to see who it was.

"What do you have to say for yourself, bear?" Captain Mandrin asked.

"Regarding what?"

"Regarding the death of my sailors. I told you under no circumstances were you to leave this cabin, and you and your three friends deliberately disobeyed my orders."

Ned caught his growl before he did or said something he would regret later. He puffed out his cheeks before releasing his breath in a long exhale. He looked to the others for some sort of answer.

"I don't understand." Ned scratched the back of his neck. "Calico was dead, and Maydia had taken over the ship. They had the entire crew at gunpoint. Seemed to me that all was lost."

"All of which we had planned for!" Mandrin punched a tankard off the table, spilling its contents into the darkness of the cabin. He sighed. "Calico's and the others' deaths are unfortunate tragedies. Those I hadn't planned on. I hadn't counted on Maydia killing Calico after he won. I did count on him stringing me up and taking over the ship. You've been cooking and vomiting the entire trip, and all of a sudden you're Bojana herself crashing through my door."

"But I saved your life."

"All you did was prematurely cause my escape. The dolphins would've made sure I wasn't shredded across the bottom of my own ship."

"I didn't know that."

"Of course you didn't."

The captain made his way across the table from Ned and sat between his two officers. Guidry was still pacing

"Just because you're a bear, I don't need to include you in all of my plans. Your orders were to remain hidden here until I called for you."

Ned stood and growled. "I saved your life!"

Everyone except the captain stood with their paws on their hilts.

"You'd draw your swords and guns on me?" *How dare they.* Ned bared his teeth. "Take your paws off your hilts. Even with just one arm, I can take all of you."

"Enough," Amina said. "Let us all take a moment and regroup and remember we're all on the same team." She leaned forward, showing him her empty paws. "Ned, we are grateful for what you did. It was foolish and wrong of us not to include you in our plans."

She motioned toward the captain. "We see that this was a mistake now."

Ned slowly sat back down. "Why didn't you tell me we were going to bring back the magic? I thought this was a treasure hunt."

"You read Labarre's clues the same as all of us." The captain leaned back and crossed his arms. "If you want my advice, don't put on any helmets when we get there. My intentions are to bring back as much gold as the hold can carry, not any magic. And, of course, we've been collecting god stones. They're the most valuable prize in the Land. Every pirate is collecting them, but you will see none aboard this ship. They're buried, hidden away until they're useful."

The captain looked away for a moment to take a deep breath. His demeanor softened when he faced Ned. "And with a little luck, we'll find my family's heirlooms that were lost at sea with my mother and father. Why a bear is needed, I don't know. But you agreed to help me, to help us. Now I fear the *Dirty Whisker* will not rest until she has taken you alive."

"I told you all this was a bad idea," Guidry said in a smug tone as he cleaned his spectacles. "We were foolish to think this treasure hunt would work. Now the bear will get us all killed."

Amina shot him a look. "Now is not the time."

"You know I'm right. You agreed with me back when the bard told us there was a bear in Wexlin."

"Get out!" the captain said. "Everyone out but Ned."

Amina, Jaja, and Guidry were slow to leave. At the captain's glare, they exited without further protest.

The captain waited until he was sure they were gone before he spoke. "Forgive me. I should have elaborated on what it means to have you aboard our ship and what dangers you will attract. Guidry and Amina, they were right from the beginning. We all took a huge risk bringing you aboard." He put his head into his paws and rubbed his eyes. "And Calico. He was right too. Maydia is not just a ghost story." He leaned closer to Ned. "But if we find this treasure, we can save an entire city full of lives."

"Only by burning it down and installing yourself as king of the ashes?"

The captain closed his eyes and sighed. "There will be a siege on the castle. Will some creatures die? Yes, an unfortunate consequence of a regime change. But change and gold are necessary. I can buy soldiers, seed, and supplies. And the commoners will benefit from it far more than the noble class."

"And what are you to do with the merchant and noble classes?" Ned was familiar with what happened during regime changes. The rich liked to continue to be rich.

"Some will fall in line with the new ways. Most will fight it. My goal is to end the social economic classes. I don't wish for there to be rich and poor. I wish for there to be a city of creatures all living in comfort."

"While we're wishing for things, I'd like to wish for a stream with an endless supply of salmon."

The captain chuckled. "Fair thing to say. Wealth and power are difficult things to yield, but the selfless and the strong know they must."

"Says the would-be king." Ned had heard stories like this before. Some creature thought they alone could fix it. But he couldn't lie to himself—it seemed different with Mandrin. Ned genuinely believed he wanted to help. He didn't understand why. Maybe because this time he wasn't fighting for a faceless king.

"Governor." Mandrin tugged at his whiskers. "I can't sit idle and let the city rot. Especially if I believe there is something I can do. The Clayborns serve nobody but themselves. I will enrich the city, restore its wealth, and rid her of its rot. Or I will do none of it. My crew has grown weary. I need you as much as you need me. An otter's loyalty wavers like the wind. I'm afraid if I lose your faith in me, then it will be all over."

Ned raised an eyebrow. "How so?"

"Without Calico here to stop them, they'll install Guidry as captain. Guidry had been a friend, but something changed in him when I brought Amina, Jaja, Calico, and the others on board." He shook his head. "He'd rather raid ships than help those who need us. And when he's captain, he'll turn the ship around back to Wexlin and hand us all over to the Clayborns for a bounty."

"Labarre wrote if I put on the helmet to restore the magic, I'll die. Or I can die when we get back to Wexlin. These are the choices that lay before me."

"It appears we need each other to stay alive. All I ask is that you trust me when I say I have both of our best interests at heart. I won't make you put on the barbute." He stuck out his paw for Ned to swipe.

A cry from the crow's nest interrupted them. "Sails! Starboard! Green sails!"

Ned and the captain jumped to their feet.

"By the luck of Cosme, there is no way." The captain pushed past Ned, spyglass in his paw. "Go to the cargo hold and hide. But stay close."

Ned lowered himself into the cargo hold but was still able to partially see what was happening on deck. The captain went to the top deck and peered through his spyglass at the pursuing ship. He whirled around and barked orders at Jaja, who turned the wheel toward the potential hostile.

Norbert had taken Pierre's place as the new war drummer. Perhaps welcoming the distraction, Norbert had embraced his new role and gleefully played the drums. With all the noise and confusion of the incoming assault, the drums were all Ned could hear.

"Secondary positions!" Guidry shouted. "Norbert!" He waited for the drums to stop. "Starboard cannons."

Norbert nodded and changed the rhythm on the drums. Ned ducked below at a familiar tapping on the small of his back.

"Is it really the ghost ship again?" Ivin tasted the air with his tongue. "How is this possible? I thought we blew it up?"

Ned scratched his neck. "It appears you can't blow up a cursed ship."

"Tino says our only hope to get away from the ghost ship is to get on land."

"I believe that is the captain's plan. Is Tino still with Pierre? How is Pierre doing?"

Ivin looked away and took a deep breath. "Pierre's gone. He went not too long ago. I'm sorry to be the one to tell you."

A sharp pain stabbed Ned's chest, and his mouth went dry. He had been optimistic that Pierre would pull through after their conversation. Tears pooled in his eyes, and it took all his strength to prevent them from turning into a river.

"Thank you for telling me," Ned said, choking out his words.

He looked away. He didn't want Ivin to see him cry. His father always used to say, "There is nothing more sad or pathetic than a grown bear crying." Those words had always haunted Ned.

"Is there anything I can do for you? I know Pierre was your friend."

Ned did his best to discreetly wipe away a tear, still trying not to look back down at Ivin. "No, but thank you for asking. Well, maybe you could stay with Tino? I don't think he'll want to be alone right now."

"Of course. What will they have you do up here?" His tongue flicked again.

"The captain asked me to stay close by."

"More fighting, I suppose."

Ned sighed. "I suppose."

Norbert still pounded the same rhythm on the drums. The crew had brought up some powder and shot to the swivel cannons, with otters in position. The captain yelled something to Guidry. Norbert stopped beating the drums.

"Fire!" Guidry shouted. "Fire!"

Norbert slammed on the drums. The cannons fired, and the floor roared and vibrated beneath Ned's feet. His ears rang, and he couldn't hear anything. When the ringing in Ned's ears stopped, Norbert was pounding a different rhythm on the drums, an intense smile on his face.

The *Ironwill* unloaded her cannons seven times by Ned's count. The *Dirty Whisker* had countered with little return fire. Ned thought they had sailed out of range until the occasional cannonball rattled the side of the *Ironwill*. Lightning flickered out of the corner of his eye. He faced the bow of the ship. To the starboard side, it was blue skies and sunshine. On the *Ironwill*'s port side was a wall of gray clouds. Lightning flashed as the wall of clouds engulfed the blue skies and crept toward the ships.

Ned's heart raced. He had never seen storm clouds like these. Cannonballs battered the deck, reminding him of the danger on both sides. On the quarterdeck, Guidry yelled at the captain, who responded by pushing his first mate away. Amina grabbed the now enraged Guidry, who charged at the captain. Guidry kicked and screamed, but Ned couldn't imagine what had gotten him so angry. The *Ironwill* changed course and headed directly into the wall of storm clouds.

"Are we steering into the clouds?" Ned asked to anyone who could hear him.

"It appears we are." Norbert sheathed his drumsticks. "I'd go tie down anything you don't want to lose. And find something that floats. We're in for a rough one."

Rain viciously sprayed from all directions. The storm clouds cloaked the ship in darkness. Waves crashed over the railing. The crew on the deck scattered. Amina grabbed the captain, and she and Kenson did everything they could to hold on to the railing. Lighting rent the sky, and even the loudest thunder couldn't block out Jaja's groans as he unsuccessfully tried to keep the wheel steady. He lost his grip, and the wheel spun wildly.

Ned knew what he had to do. He climbed out of the cargo hold and dug his claws into the wooden planks of the deck. Each step was a battle. The *Ironwill* rocked and swayed, water coming at him from all directions. He put his head down and tried to cut his way through the heavy wind pushing him back. When he got closer to the ladder, the captain and Amina shouted for him to go back. He didn't care. He had to help Jaja.

When Ned finally reached the wheel, Jaja collapsed from exhaustion. His arms fell lifelessly to his sides. Ned grabbed the wheel, which did all it could to spin. His arm burned and throbbed as he steadied the wheel. He growled as blood seeped through his bandage. Through the darkness of the rain, he saw a light on the horizon. He pointed the ship in that direction, as it seemed like the logical choice. It was as if the ocean showed him the way.

Ned used all of his strength to keep the wheel steady, but it wasn't enough. His arms and chest burned as it tried to spin out of his paws. His left arm felt useless. Maybe if he could use both arms, this would be easier. He roared, straining to keep the wheel steady and toward the sun patch ahead.

"Jaja will help you!"

Jaja stood alongside him, and together they steadied the wheel. They would be out of this storm in a short time. Hopefully the *Dirty Whisker* hadn't followed them.

"Stop! Let it spin! You're going to—"

Before the captain could finish, the mast creaked, then snapped. Splintering wood fell from the sky. The center mast unnaturally swayed until the crow's nest broke off with a thunderous crack.

The top of the mast crashed through the rigging. Ned wasn't sure what to do. The crow's nest was tangled in ropes and sails, which kept it from falling. A weight lifted off his chest but quickly dropped into his stomach. The broken mast swung down toward him. Without thinking, he tried to catch it. He steadied his grip on the wooden planks to brace for the impact. With a *thud*, the mast swung into him, and to his surprise, he caught it with relative ease.

Falling debris struck his head. Ned collapsed to the deck, the broken mast falling on top of him.

# Chapter 12
# The Calm

Ten days had passed since the *Ironwill* sailed through the storm. Ned had fully recovered, though he could still feel a bump on his head. He had been dizzy and nauseous, but he had been fortunate to have not suffered a broken bone. But the wound on his arm had grown worse. He did his best to keep it clean, but it was starting to pus and hurt every time he moved it.

The ship had lost most of her center mast and canvas. It had taken the crew an entire day to sew together the remnants of the sails. The *Ironwill* was able to catch some wind, but they were moving at a frighteningly slow pace. Still, there had been no sign of the *Dirty Whisker*.

Ned worried they'd run out of food before they made it to land. He had been scraping the bottoms of their barrels every evening. Luka and Vesna restocked their stores after their daily hunts with the dolphins, but that was only enough for the next day. They had no surplus.

"The bear and gorilla get enough food to feed eight otters," Ned overheard the otter gunner Clovis say after the third day.

From then on, Ned went without food some days. When his

hunger raged, he'd eat a small fish to try to tame it. Ivin also stopped taking his rations. He consumed the flies that lingered aboard. Ned did his best to stretch the ingredients out even further, but now all the vegetables and roots were gone. He still had a full spice pack, and he had time, so he made the best-tasting meals with what little he had.

Against the entire crew's wishes, Ned did not allow them to send Pierre's body out to sea. He helped them wrap Pierre in seaweed and canvas like the others. He told them Pierre's final wishes, but the crew insisted it was tradition. Instead, Ned placed his friend's body into a barrel of spiced rum that Calico had given him.

The barrels of liquor and fresh drinking water were getting low, and when Guidry asked Ned to share his barrel of spiced rum, he didn't know how to tell him he had preserved Pierre in it. With each day, simple tasks like sitting up required all of Ned's strength. Walking and staying awake were now daunting tasks. He gave himself no reason to endure. Despite how hot it was, he spent most of his time in his cot, avoiding the others. He only wished he had more water.

Ned had grown tired of the crew. He once thought of them as friends. Now the nicer otters avoided eye contact with him, while the others not so discreetly discussed how they wished the captain had never brought a bear aboard.

"I thought he was here to protect us, not get us killed," one otter said.

"If we weren't feeding a bear, we wouldn't need to be on rations," another said.

Even Tino and Norbert stopped talking to him for not burying Pierre at sea, both insisting they never heard Pierre say he wanted a different funeral. Jaja and the other officers tried to find a way to get the *Ironwill* sailing faster. All there was left to do was sit alone in his room and wish for time to move faster. Maybe this was why Calico had hidden in his room all the time.

# Ned Bear

Ned's stomach groaned to remind him he was starving. He decided he was going to eat his full rations tonight and maybe Ivin's too if the iguana still insisted on eating just flies. He scratched his leg. His breeches were loose, and he had to tie them around his waist with rope from the old rigging. Between Goran's revenge at the beginning of the journey and not eating now, he had grown weak and skinny. He lifted his good arm to grab his pack, but he was too frail to maintain his grip. The pack crashed to the floor. He lay back down. He'd pick everything up another day.

Ned let out a sigh. He had dreams of exploring the world like the great Ulrich Leon Labarre, writing his own books, and becoming the most famous bear explorer the Land had ever known. Maybe young bear cubs would read about his journeys and travel the world instead of killing each other over whichever banner or king they were under. If he were to die, would his mother ever find out? Would she go looking for answers, or was she ashamed that he was a deserter? Maybe if he found the treasure, he could go back home. Perhaps gold coin and riches would buy his family's forgiveness.

"If we ever find the treasure," he mumbled. "We were closer to it when we were in Wexlin."

He tried to remove his journal from his pack, but it was out of reach, and he lacked the strength to get out of bed. He closed his eyes, trying to recall what he could about the notes he had made about their journey. It didn't matter. He couldn't shake what Pierre had told him before he died—how Labarre had watched bears put on Bojana's barbute and die. How could Labarre do that? How could he knowingly send so many bears to their deaths? Was he that heartless, or did he truly believe it would work even after so many failed attempts?

If Labarre really knew all the steps, why didn't he restore the magic? What was he hiding? Perhaps he didn't bring back the magic because he was worried about the harm it would cause? Questions continued to swirl in Ned's head. Would he even want to bring the magic back if he could? If Labarre didn't bring back the treasure, was it even real?

Ivin poked his head up the ladder into Ned's quarters. "They're back from the hunt."

With serious effort and a groan, Ned sat up and went to greet Luka. The room seemed to spin as he stood. Luka waited in the galley with a sour expression that made it clear what he was about to say before he said it.

"There were no schools in the water. We'll try again after the dolphins rest."

He nodded at Ned, and Ned returned it, hoping Luka didn't hear his stomach growling. Luka left, and news of the unsuccessful hunt spread fast. The otters chirped and barked, clearly upset.

"You should see what all that is about," Ivin said.

Ned knew what it was about, but he also knew Ivin was terrified they'd come for him. Since Maydia's parley, the otters' hostility had grown toward Ivin, and he no longer slept with the crew. Ned suspected they were taking their frustration with him out on Ivin. When Ned suggested they do something about it, Ivin waved it off and said it was best for them not to poke the hornets' nest. Instead, he slept in the galley or at the foot of Ned's bed, refusing to sleep in Calico's empty bed.

Ned climbed the ladder to the top deck, and the chatter died down. The sun was blinding with the ship missing most of her sails. He looked for shade but found none.

"There he is." Jaja pointed down at Ned from the quarterdeck. "Tell him. If you otters are so certain he's the problem, tell him."

"I take orders from the captain, not you!" Guidry shouted at Jaja. "You're all part of the problem. If it wasn't for you monsters, we'd have enough food. And we wouldn't be starving!"

The otters all cheered.

"Guidry!" Amina stepped forward from behind Jaja. "Cease this madness, and prepare the ship for sleep."

Guidry stood tall, his face twisted into a snarl. "Quiet, dog! I don't take orders from you either."

The crowd's jeers and applause were cut short when Amina kicked Guidry in the torso, sending him over the railing to the lower deck. Some of the crew tried to catch him, but they merely slowed his fall to the deck.

"When the captain isn't on deck, I am your captain!" Amina yelled. "I will not remind you all of that again!"

A hush fell over the crew. They lowered their heads, their eyes darting around. It appeared the fight had been kicked out of them for now.

"Every time we run into trouble, you blame those who aren't otters," Amina said. "How many times are we going to have this fight? Is this fight going to bring us food? Ned isn't causing us to starve. We're not causing you to starve. Two abandoned stops, a gunfight, a storm, and a broken mast are causing you to starve. Now find something productive to do." She spat on the deck and walked away.

The otters, heads down and tails dragging, dispersed. Guidry held his stomach during a fit of coughing. He glanced around. With the help of a few otters, he rose and walked away like nothing had happened.

A gentle breeze fluttered through Ned's fur. It wasn't enough to move the *Ironwill*, but it was something. He flared his nostrils and extended his neck as high as he could, trying to catch as much of the wind as possible. Something squawked. He shook his head. Was his brain playing a trick on him, or did he really hear a gull? The entire crew was frozen in place on the top deck. Did they hear it too? This time two squawks pierced the air. It was the sound of triumph, the sound of a gull. They were close to shore.

# Chapter 13
# The Stranger

Much to Ned's displeasure, the captain decided to dock on the abandoned north side of the island of Tortue. Jaja explained that with a damaged *Ironwill*, the crew on the verge of starvation, and being hunted by the *Dirty Whisker*, it was their only choice. Ned didn't like it. He would have preferred to dock in the harbor to be able to resupply, but he agreed it was probably the best thing to do. They would've been a target for any pirate looking to make easy coin.

Ned, along with just about every member of the crew, was surprised the island they happened to float to was Tortue. They weren't completely lost. Once the ship was secure, most of the crew jumped off the sides into the shallows to search for something to eat in the reefs. Ned thought of doing the same, but he didn't want to get his bandages wet. His arm still ached, and he wasn't even sure he had the strength to lift his legs over the railing to get into the water. Instead, he waited for his turn to be lowered down in the boat and to be paddled ashore with his pack of journals and spices and the barrel of spiced rum to be buried.

It was nearly nightfall when he rowed ashore with Ivin. Ned

gingerly sipped at the water sack Ivin had, trying not to take too much of the water for himself. He passed it back to Ivin, who slurped it eagerly. The captain had given them a day and two nights to find food and to do as they pleased.

Ned wasn't sure he'd return to the ship. He didn't know if he could trust the captain even though he still believed in his cause. He wanted to help him save Wexlin, but he wasn't certain the captain truly had his best interests at heart. He hated feeling like a pawn in someone else's game. Ned and Ivin didn't feel welcome by the crew, and after seeing how fast they turned on them both when things got tough, Ned knew they would've killed Ivin for food if he wasn't aboard. He didn't really see a reason for them to go back.

From the rowboat, Tortue seemed peaceful. Crystal-blue water rushed onto white sand beaches. The otters reported the reefs provided ample fish and shellfish. Many who had jumped overboard were already asleep on the beach with full bellies by the time Ned arrived.

Ned did not want to camp on the beach with the crew. With his pack over his shoulder and the barrel under his arm, he pushed through the thick underbrush of the jungle as the sun set behind him. He stopped about every hundred yards and listened for a stream. He mostly heard the tapping of Ivin's claws as he followed close behind. Ivin's head darted back and forth as he searched the underbrush. He looked over at the setting sun and frowned.

Even with Ivin's claws tapping close behind and Ned's stomach growling loudly, Ned heard a stream. He darted off his original path and pushed through the jungle toward the sound of running water. Just before the sun disappeared below the island's mountains, they found a grassy patch where the water trickled by.

The grass was perfect for a camp. It was soft, and the area was mostly flat. Upstream there was a large pool that gradually overflowed as the source. Ned expected a huge waterfall to be filling the lagoon, but there was none. Tears welled up in his eyes when he saw plenty of large fish in the lagoon and stream.

"Any danger?" Ivin flicked his tongue.

"Not that I can see. This place seems almost too perfect." Ned collapsed next to Ivin as he worked on a fire.

Ivin banged the two fire stones together. "What about food?"

"I'd have to make a spear or slap them up onto shore." Ned turned onto his back in the tall grass, his gaze falling on the spiced rum barrel. "Let me rest a moment before I get in the water."

"I could look for some fruit or smaller game."

"No need for that. I'll get in the stream in a moment."

It was night, yet it remained light out. The purple clouds floating through the orange sky made it feel like the sun was setting for hours. A rustling in the high grass stirred Ned out of his daze.

Ivin's eyes widened. "You hear that?"

Ned motioned for him to be quiet and rolled onto his side as quietly as he could. The rustling surged toward him at an alarming pace. He lay still and waited for the tall grass to split and for his predator to emerge. It was a wild hog about the size of a small bison. How could one so big live on this island for so long?

The hog snarled and snorted at Ned before turning its attention to Ivin. Ivin froze, his body trembling. The boar lowered its head and charged at Ivin, who screamed and ran. Ned sprang up to catch the beast. As its tusks inched toward Ivin, Ned punched the hog on the side of its head. It squealed and fell onto its side, sliding into the grass. Ned snarled and shook his paw. He had caught the hard part of the boar's head.

The boar kicked its legs and regained its footing, then charged at Ned. Ned stood tall and growled, but the hog didn't seem to notice. It lowered its tusks and tried to gore Ned's knee as he had anticipated. Ned jumped, pulled his leg away, and landed on top of the hog. The boar bucked and squealed. Ned's arm burned as he tried to hold the beast. He roared and drove his claws into its throat. It let out a dreadful squeal. Blood poured down Ned's paw.

Ivin's gaze darted around the tall grass. "If anyone was looking for us, they'll certainly find us now."

Ned placed the hog in front of Ivin and washed his paws in the stream. He built a spit for the boar to be cooked over the fire. The smell of the cooked pork was intoxicating. The smoke was rich and sweet, adding flavor to the meat, and Ned's mouth was already watering. He was so hungry that he tore pieces off the hog and ate them when they were only slightly kissed by the fire. For the first time since he had boarded the *Ironwill*, he had a full belly. The fire dwindled over the bones of the wild hog as he thought about lying in the tall grass for a much-needed nap.

"Best be moving on now. You killed one of the queen's hogs. They'll send the brigade for you." An old sea otter in a dark-green cloak, both paws leaning on a wooden walking stick, stood in the tall grass just outside their makeshift camp.

Fire shot through Ned's veins as he sat up. *How did this old otter sneak up on me?* "Who are you?"

The old sea otter pulled off his green hood to reveal his face. It had grayed from age, which accented his piercing seaweed-colored eyes. "A friend. Now gather your things, and I'll show you where you need to be."

The otter ambled away. Ned looked at Ivin, who shrugged. Ned gathered his things and the leftover meat from the hog. He buried what was left, put out the fire, and followed the old sea otter.

"Where are you taking us, stranger?" Ned hurried to keep pace with the otter as they made their way up the slope of the mountain.

"A place with a view."

Ivin ran to keep up. "I thought you said you were taking us away from the queen's guard?"

The stranger didn't answer. The trail was narrow and weaved in and out of the tropical trees. The trees twisted and turned like they danced with one another, sprouting to create a green canopy over the trail. Among the various ferns was the occasional traditional-looking tree trunk that was wide and went straight up. These trunks had bark with vibrant stripes of red, yellow, orange, and blue.

"Fire tree." Without slowing down, the otter pointed at one with his walking stick.

Ned's chest burned as he gasped for air. He'd never been this tired from just walking before. His legs collapsed out from under him, which caused him to stumble forward and drop the barrel of rum. The barrel rolled back down the trail. Ned grabbed for it, but it was just out of reach. He begged it to stop rolling, but it was starting to pick up speed.

Ned's lower jaw dropped so hard it nearly fell off when Ivin jumped in front of the barrel and stopped it. It easily weighed as much as he did.

"Thank you." Ned panted and grabbed the barrel. "I can't believe you were able to stop it."

"Been moving and rolling barrels twice as heavy as this at the market." Ivin sat next to him. "How is that old otter not tired?" He nodded in the direction of the old otter, who was still walking.

They both rested to gather their strength. Being on the ship and not eating a real meal until today had taken a toll on their ability to walk.

The stranger was well out of sight now. He didn't turn around nor slow his pace. When Ned and Ivin had the energy to move again, they continued up the trail.

"We could always turn back," Ivin said.

"It can't be too much farther."

At the top of the mountain, the otter looked over the grand valley, his robes fluttering in the wind. Ned and Ivin stood beside him.

The trees and clouds that had already fallen into darkness gave off a shade of purple that contrasted with the vibrant orange sky. The endless sun highlighted the red cliff that rose up above the emerald jungle canopy. The jungle grew thick in the valley, like it was an overflowing liquid held in place by the surrounding mountains. The city of Tortue sat nestled in the jungle by the bay of the blue ocean. Tall ships drifted in and out of the harbor like ants returning to the hill. A single gray pyramid in the center of the valley interrupted the flow of green.

"Do you know what this place is?" the otter asked. "There used to be magic. Sorcerers, wizards, mages, and shamans all ventured to this place. Balancing the forces of nature, balancing life. Working with the gods to protect those who needed protection. A passageway between realms. Now it's just the jungle." He frowned.

"What happened?" Ned asked.

"Bojana. Bojana locked it all away with her power."

"Her power was the barbute," Ivin said. "The helmet was the source of her power."

The stranger raised an eyebrow. "Her helmet was her helmet. What do you know of this?"

"I heard it in a song," Ivin said. "Does Goran have the helmet?"

The otter studied Ivin before glaring at Ned. "The barbute is useless unless it's worn by a bear. A willing and worthy one. Bury your friend anywhere up here. He'll have a view fit for a king." He turned away.

"Wait. How did you know? And where will you go?" Ned asked.

Without answering, the otter vanished into the jungle.

"Are we really going to bury Pierre here?" Ivin asked. "You think it's a trick of some sort?"

"Would be a strange trick or trap. Why lead us all that way? If he meant us any harm, he wouldn't have woken us up."

"I suppose you're right. I find it odd he led us to this spot. And that he knew what was in the barrel. I don't remember either of us telling him."

Ned grunted. "I don't know how he knew. I also don't see what difference it makes. He was right. This is the perfect place. The ground is soft enough, and there are plenty of flat stones around. Just look at this place. Pierre would have loved it."

All the guilt he had gotten from the crew for not burying Pierre with the others vanished when Ned started digging. It would've been easy for him to have gone along with the others, but he had needed to try to do what Pierre wanted. His chest no longer ached when he looked at the rum barrel; instead, it only lifted his spirits to dig faster. Ivin gathered flat stones, the biggest ones he could lift. The ground was soft dirt that easily ripped up with each pass from Ned's claws. When he had gotten the hole large and deep enough for the barrel, he helped Ivin gather stones.

Ivin froze. "You hear something?"

Ned had not heard anything. He held his breath and tilted his head. Ivin extended his neck to listen better.

"I don't hear anything. What did you hear, Ivin?"

Faint otter chatter drifted up the trail. Someone from the crew had followed them. Ivin moved behind Ned, his tail nervously tapping the ground. Norbert and Tino made their way into the clearing.

"Oy. How'd you find us?" Ned asked.

"I told you we were almost there." Tino slapped Norbert's belly. "Ned, we're glad to see you."

"Some old sea otter told us where to find you." Norbert tossed Ned his water sack. "We were filling up water sacks 'cause things were getting pretty intense with the crew on the beach. This old otter snuck up on us and insisted we follow him to find you."

"Well, I'm glad you found us. Just in time, I believe." Ned nodded at the hole with the stones stacked near the barrel.

Both otters sighed and looked away.

"Good," Tino said through tears. "Let us all say goodbye together."

Norbert lit four torches he had made from driftwood, beach tar, and lamp oil and set them in the ground around the hole. The camp glowed orange from the fire as Ned removed Pierre from his temporary home in the spiced rum barrel and placed him in the ground. When they had finished covering Pierre, Tino threw dirt over the flat stones to create a dirt mound and stacked sticks on top of it. He placed so many so tightly together that they formed a table.

He put four tin cups on Pierre's table and poured them each a drink from his flask. Ned sniffed the cup. It was rum, which made him smirk. He looked at the rum barrel that had been Pierre's temporary resting place. He would probably always think of Pierre when he smelled rum from now on.

"Been saving my rations for this. Such a fine resting place," Tino said.

"He hated the sea." Norbert snorted. "He only stayed on the *Ironwill* for us. This was the right thing to do, Ned." He wiped away a tear. "I'm sorry we were angry with you before."

"We just wanted to give a proper send-off and didn't think this could happen. Thought we'd only see the snow island and didn't want to leave him in the cold." Tino sniffed. "I wish you would have really gotten to know him."

Ned wished he would have had that chance too. In his short time with Pierre, he had grown to trust him.

"I've never had any real friends." Ned spun his cup. "It's difficult for bears. It's hard to trust when you're constantly treated as a weapon. Some bears have an easier time with it than others. I never have." He finished his drink. "Pierre never asked for anything from me other than an ear to listen, and in return, he offered his to me. I only knew him for a short while, but he was my friend. Now a journey for gold seems foolish. Pierre never got to go home. He deserved better." Tears welled in his eyes, and his head hurt from fighting them back. "I'll give you some time alone while I go set up camp." He did his best to keep his voice steady.

When he was far enough away, Ned began to sob.

# Chapter 14
# The Puzzle

Ned's arm ached from lying on it awkwardly, and it woke him. His mouth dry, he was afraid even his entire sack of water wouldn't quench his thirst. He tried to remember if he had seen a creek nearby, but thinking made his head hurt. He decided it was best to roll over, go back to sleep, and try waking up again later.

Ned, Ivin, and Tino were comfortable with sleeping the morning away when Norbert uncharacteristically ran back into the camp.

"Ned! Tino! Wake up!" Norbert shouted, tying his trousers.

"Quiet, Berty." Tino moaned. "We're not making you breakfast."

"No time for that now. You have to come see this!"

Ned sat up. He couldn't believe Norbert said there was no time for breakfast and ran. He needed to see what he was talking about.

Not far from their makeshift camp was a stone building with a black tiled roof and a small stone door. Ned recognized it as a tomb right away. He'd seen plenty of them in Wexlin, but this one was far grander. A superior stone cutter chiseled and perfectly stacked the stones ten feet high with hardly any mortar used. It was big enough to be a small church. *Who or what is buried in there?*

Norbert had found this tomb, and if there was even a small possibility of danger, he would've been running in the other direction. Instead, he put his paw on the door, and Ned sucked in a breath. What if the place was booby-trapped?

"The key is a sleepless bear." Norbert pointed at an engraved name above the door. "We're standing at the tomb of Ulrich Labarre." He cracked a big smile and stepped back.

Ned fell to the ground, placed both paws on top of his head, and started laughing. The tomb of the explorer who led them on this crazy journey. He ran his paw over the name chiseled into the stone—Ulrich Leon Labarre. Everyone assumed he had been lost at sea, the great explorer overtaken by the ocean. When in truth, he never left Tortue.

"Look at the door," Norbert said eagerly.

The door was stone like the rest of the tomb but had claw marks and divots around the frame. There had been attempts to open it with no success. Around the door were seven light-gray spheres with sigils Ned recognized immediately. They were the round seals on the covers of each of Labarre's books.

"Watch this." Norbert stretched up to remove the one closest to him.

He tossed it into some grass nearby. It shot out of the grass and placed itself back on the tomb.

"It's a sorcerer's door," Norbert said. "And you said Labarre may have traveled with a sorceress. And look in the center of the door. It's sized for only a bear claw. A bear is the key!"

Norbert was right. Ned cautiously placed his claws into the door. He held his breath, expecting the door to jump out at him. His claws locked into place, and the stone jiggled. He tried to turn it left, then right, but the stone merely clicked.

Ned stepped away. "It didn't work."

"Good." Tino sighed. "Tomb raiding is for raccoons."

"Don't forget about a dead otter's curse," Ivin said.

"You don't see it?" Norbert chuckled. "The gods and Labarre have brought Ned here. Captain might know where Goran's new island is, but we were always supposed to come here first."

Ned remembered a conversation he had with Calico before Maydia attacked.

"Calico thought the same thing." Ned searched his pack for the parchments. "There was a parchment with a picture of the tomb. Aye, here it is." He handed it to Norbert.

Norbert studied it. "Take the bear on a turtle's back. It's written right here. *Tortue* means 'turtle' in otter. This has to be it."

"Then why couldn't you open the door?" Ivin asked.

"I don't know. There has to be a reason I couldn't get in." Ned searched for some sort of clue.

Norbert scratched his dark chin hairs and squinted at the door. "Whatever is inside here should give us the answers. It's quite clever when you think about it. The clue was so direct it was mysterious. 'A bear is the key.'"

"Maybe there is another clue in the riddle," Ivin said.

Ned pulled out his journal where he had made a copy of Labarre's treasure riddle. He had studied it intensely but had grown frustrated after making no progress.

*I alone had made it there*
*To the land of treasures bold*
*My path will show you where*
*To make a new world from the old*
*Journey south until it's north*
*Tucked in ice you'll find a jungle there*
*Alone you cannot go forth*
*The key is a sleepless bear*
*Take the bear on a turtle's back*
*To marvel at my life's quest*
*For riches too grand for any sack*

# Ned Bear

*In success all shall be blessed*

"How are we going to open this door?" Norbert asked.

Tino backed away from the tomb. "Berty, I don't think messing with a sorcerer's door, especially one guarding the dead, is a good idea."

"I agree," Ivin said.

"We're not poking around his bones," Norbert said. "Look at the size of this thing. All this for one river otter? Ned was meant to open this door. Now, help me figure this out."

"They're not just drawings." Ned pointed at all of his Labarre books in the grass. "Those seals are on the covers of all his books."

Norbert returned his attention to the sepulcher. "Why would he put his book covers on his tomb?"

Tino's eyes darted around. "We should leave and not touch it any further."

"Go wait back at camp if you're so scared." Norbert eyed the door. "Ned and I are going to see about opening this door. What about you, Ivin?"

"I'll meet you all back at the camp." Ivin hurried away.

Tino sat as far away as he could while still being able to observe.

"Norbert, do you think the spheres line up in a linear formation?" Ned scanned the wall. "What order do we put them in?"

"It's the third line of the poem," Ivin yelled back to them, his head poking around a tree.

"The third line?" Ned searched the poem again. "Here it is. 'My path will show you where.' What path?"

Norbert and Ned surveyed the tomb, hoping an answer would reveal itself. They stood in silence, scratching their heads.

"Does the wall look like a map to you?" Norbert said.

Ned tilted his head. The wall was the map of the world. It all made sense now.

"To marvel at my life's quest," Ned said, mirroring the riddle. "I believe we've discovered another step."

"I'm not following," Norbert said.

Ned grabbed the tile with the human paw on it and placed it in the Swallowed Sea where Labarre first landed in the Land of Only Man. The tile vibrated in his paw, and when he let go, the tile glowed blue and stayed locked in place.

"That did something." Norbert grinned. "You think we have to put them in some sort of order?"

"I think we should follow his journey." Ned scratched his chin. "He went to the Land of the Barbarians and then around the cape up to the Sea Otter Islands."

Ned grabbed the tile with ocean waves for the Land of the Barbarians and inserted it in the east coast where Labarre had landed. Next was the trident for the Sea Otter Islands, and he set that one on Cuwar Island off the west coast of the Land. The tiles responded the same as the previous one, first vibrating before glowing blue and locking into place.

Ned couldn't help but chuckle. "I believe we've figured this out."

He put the tiger tile on the east coast of the land mass on the far edge of the map that had large mountain ranges for the places unexplored. It was across the Sunset Sea from Cuwar Island and had been one of Labarre's longer stops but the least explored. Next, he placed the giant lizard claw on the east coast of the large island to the far south of the Sunset Sea.

The sixth tile was the flightless bird Labarre called a penguin, which he set on the Island of Winter on the southern edge of the map in the bay Ned had been calling Treasure Cove. His heart raced. Only one more to go—a quill from Labarre's final book.

Where did this go? Ned knew it was from the cover of Labarre's memoirs. He had gotten the book from Mama but hadn't read it yet. His mouth was dry, and his tongue fell out when his uncontrollable panting started.

"Put it on Wexlin," Norbert said. "That's the only place it could go."

Not having a better idea, Ned took a deep breath and placed the final tile on Wexlin. Once it locked in, the bear claw on the door glowed blue. Ned took a deep breath and stuck his claws into the slots.

"Here goes nothing," he said as he gave it a twist.

The claw lock easily turned, and the entire map illuminated brighter than a morning sun. Ned stepped back, squinting and shielding his face from the light.

The sound of grinding rock made him turn away from the tomb and cover his ears. It hadn't been long when he decided to open his eyes. The light was gone. He turned back around to see that the crypt and map had dimmed. Now there was only the vast darkness of where the door used to be.

Ned smiled. "We did it! We opened the sorceress's door!" He picked Norbert up and hugged him.

"I can't believe it," Norbert said. "I completely guessed where to put that last tile. Then when the light started, I thought we were goners for sure!"

Ned dropped Norbert, who harmlessly tumbled into the grass.

"You guessed?" Ned said. "We could've died!"

"I know." Norbert giggled. "But it worked!"

Ned couldn't stop himself from laughing with Norbert. Almost dying didn't seem to matter. He thought about all the bears back home who teased him for reading instead of swinging his axes in the field. The teachers from his bear school who told him he'd never be anything but a weapon. His father who put a spear in his paw as soon as he could walk. All the wealthy creatures of the Land who had spent years and coin trying to solve Labarre's riddle, only to fail. If they could all see him now. A bear with no titles or land, just pure determination and curiosity, had solved one of the greatest puzzles of all time. He had found and opened Labarre's tomb, bringing them closer to the treasure of all things lost at sea.

# Chapter 15
# The Tomb

Darkness loomed before Ned, the air in the tomb stale. His chest tightened as he sucked in a breath, the hair on his back standing on end.

"I can't see anything," he said.

"Here you go." Norbert handed him a torch he had to pinch between two claws. "You go ahead."

Ned squinted into the darkness. "This is barely doing anything."

He thought the tomb looked larger on the inside than the outside. Its rectangular shape reminded him of an empty feasting hall. Once he crossed the threshold, he was able to stand up with plenty of head room. He started to shake, and he wasn't as excited about being here. He expected magical traps and didn't know if his first step onto the stone floor would be his last. He had read the stories. He knew all about Labarre's encounters with traps set by sorcerers. Sorcerers were known to have a morbid sense of humor and took pride in finding creative ways to kill creatures.

He waved the torch in front of him to try to get a better view of the tomb before entering any farther, but the flame was too small for him to make sense of anything.

"What do you see?" Norbert asked.

"Nothing yet." Ned's words echoed in the tomb.

"Then go on. Let me get a look."

"I'm worried the sorcerer cursed the floor."

Norbert's eyes widened. "I hadn't thought of that. I'll wait."

Ned gave the torch another wave in front of him. He found a relatively big chunk of rubble that had fallen off one of the walls. He cautiously placed it on the tile in front of him. Labarre had done the same when searching a tomb in his book *Sea Otter Islands*. He grimaced, expecting the weight of the rock to trigger a trap like poisoned darts or a fire spray. Labarre wrote that one of the stones turned into a snake and swallowed the rock he had set on it.

When nothing happened, Ned picked up the piece of rubble. He methodically put it on the three rows of three tiles in front of him. It didn't trigger any traps. When he could not reach the fourth row from the doorway, he decided it was time to take a real step into the tomb. He tapped his paw on the stone like he was testing the temperature of the river. He closed his eyes, took a deep breath, and stepped onto the first two rows of tiles.

He flinched, expecting an axe to fall. When nothing happened, he opened his eyes and looked around. There was a large torch nearly eye level on the wall that was too large for anyone to carry. He lit it with his small one.

The old torch sparked from the flame's kiss, but the light was different. Sparks of yellow, purple, blue, and green spit and fell to the floor like a fountain until a large green burst shot up the ceiling. Light from the flame burst illuminated the tomb. A green fireball shot from the torch up to the ceiling and back to the opposite wall, lighting another torch. It poured out a fountain of colorful sparks before a green fireball in the form of a hawk soared across the tomb to light two hanging lanterns above the sarcophagus.

The four green flames faded to a normal torch flame. The tomb was now lit like a common parlor. Ned's heartbeat finally slowed to a manageable pace. He rolled the rock across the tiles to be certain the floor was secure. His mouth wide open, Norbert tiptoed in through the doorway.

The flames illuminated the walls to reveal a tiled mosaic of a large ship. Not just any ship, but the infamous ship of Ulrich Leon Labarre, the *Pelican*. Many small tiles made up the grand piece of artwork no one else had seen. Ned found himself speechless. He was awestruck by the mosaic's beauty and wondered how Labarre had gotten one of the world's greatest artists all the way down here to craft this for him. He started to count the crests in one of the waves, but once he got to forty-eight, he decided there were far too many to count.

"This picture must be made up of a million little pieces," Ned said.

It appeared every detail of the multideck, three-masted galleon was there—all the sails, riggings, and cannons. Even the hanging lanterns had orange, red, and blue tiles to make up the flames.

"Wow." Norbert gave a long whistle. "Can you believe this? They must've spent a decade making this thing."

"Yes. But why?" Ned shook his head.

"Pierre always thought Labarre was in love with his own legend." Norbert wiped his eyes. "If he would've seen this, there would've been no shutting him up."

They crept farther into the tomb. Ned tested each row of tiles by tiptoeing on each and pressing them down before moving forward. Just ahead lay the sarcophagus of Labarre. It was plain, unpainted marble with a statue of him laid to rest as the lid. His sarcophagus was elevated off the ground by stone pillars in front of another marble statue of a sea otter.

The sea otter was dressed in what would have been sharkskin armor and was holding a trident. His face looked familiar even carved with a stoic look. *Where do I know that face from?* His free paw was held out as if welcoming you to slide your pad over his. Two grand columns connected by an arch held the roof over the statue that stood just as tall as the mosaic, which was more than twice as tall as Ned.

"That's Goran," Norbert said. "Why would Labarre build a temple to Goran for his tomb?"

Ned looked around the tomb with a different perspective. It was indeed more of a small chapel to Goran than a large tomb. "Why did Labarre build such a small, elaborate chapel that no one could open?"

Norbert shrugged.

Ned stepped forward, and the tile sank beneath his paw. The sound of rocks scraping against one another emitted from the statue of Goran. The statue lifted its trident off the ground and slammed the blunt end down.

"Run," Ned said.

They fled toward the open door. It slammed shut. Drops of water echoed in the small chamber until water rapidly poured from the ceiling. Within a couple of heartbeats, it had reached Ned's knees.

"What are we going to do?" Norbert screamed as the water surged up to his chin.

"I don't know. Look for a way out."

Ned tried to break open the door. He kicked, slammed, and pushed with all his might. It never budged. The water covered his chest now, submerging the door. His heart pounded, and he was having trouble breathing. He glanced around in confusion. Norbert swam in circles, searching for a way out.

"What are we going to do?" Norbert asked, out of breath.

Ned paddled to keep his head above water. "I'm sorry, Norbert. I don't know what to do. I'm sorry."

"No! This can't be it!"

Tears filled Ned's eyes. "I'm sorry."

"No. This isn't how it ends for us." Norbert dove under the water again.

The water rose above the torches, and they went out with a hiss. Ned tried to stay afloat in the complete darkness. All he could do was wait. Wait until his head hit the ceiling and then fell below the waterline. He stuck his arm up, and his paw struck the ceiling. His heart sank. It wouldn't be long now until the tomb was full of water. He sighed and closed his eyes. He punched at the ceiling, hoping he could break through, but it was solid stone. There was nothing more he could do. His head spun, and he couldn't stop himself from sobbing. If only he would've said goodbye to his mama.

His whole body was shaking, and he was bawling when his head hit the ceiling. Wherever the water had been pouring in from was submerged, as the noise had stopped. Nearby splashing interrupted the silent darkness.

"Ned!" Norbert said. "I found a way out."

"Where? How?"

"There are two glowing bear claws down there. Just like the door. I didn't see them until it got dark. It's a sorcerer's spell."

Ned looked down but saw only blackness. "I don't see any light." He tilted his head to keep his nose above the waterline.

"There's one by the statue and one under Labarre's coffin."

"Which one do I turn?"

"The Goran one? I don't know, but his trident started the flood. Grab my tail, and I'll guide you down there." Norbert got closer to him. "Don't pull my tail. You're going to have to swim yourself. I'm not paddling us both down there."

Ned grabbed Norbert's tail. They took one last deep breath and dove into the blackness. Ned tried to open his eyes to follow Norbert, but the salt water burned. Norbert swam slowly enough that it was easy for Ned to keep up. In what felt like only a couple of kicks, they had swum back down to the tile floor. Ned extended his paw and felt the sarcophagus of Labarre. Norbert pushed toward the statue of Goran. Ned didn't think he could hold his breath much longer. His lungs ached, and the wound on his arm throbbed. Whatever he needed to do, he needed to do it fast. He was starting to feel dizzy, and he was losing sensation in his toes.

Ned first felt the blunt end, then the paw of the statue. Norbert stopped swimming. He grabbed Ned's paw and set it on the claw holes. Ned peeked around. A faint blue glow outlined the claw. The weight of the world lifted off his shoulders. He inserted his claws in the holes and moved them like he had with the outside door.

It refused to turn. He struggled, twisting it back and forth, but the lock would not budge. He anchored his legs and used his free hand to help his right paw turn the key over. Nothing. His chest burned like a bison had sat on him. His head swirled. It took all of his willpower just to stay awake. He remembered Norbert had seen two glowing claw keys. He reached under the raised sarcophagus and felt for the other claw key. He inserted his claws. Nothing.

The water was calm enough that he heard Norbert thrashing. Ned's chest felt like it was on fire. Out of sheer desperation, he inserted both his claws into the two keys. When he had mere seconds of air left, he turned both claws at the same time. They both turned with ease. The floor sucked at his fur, draining the water.

Ned needed air now. With his last bit of strength, he pulled himself off the tiles. The force of the emptying water ripped his fur out. The current was too strong. Fighting for his life, he forced himself to sit up.

The water had already drained down past Ned's head. He gasped for air, coughing and trying to take deep breaths at the same time. After a few moments, only puddles rested on the uneven tiles. A subtle drip from the statue of Goran echoed throughout the darkness. Norbert chuckled. Ned started laughing too. Dodging death was not a laughing matter, yet he couldn't help it.

The tomb door slid open to reveal the silhouette of a familiar otter.

"You fellas all right?" Tino shouted.

"We are now," Ned said, catching his breath.

"What's so funny? You playing tricks on me?"

"No. Just cheated death again." Norbert wiped water away from his eyes. "It seems the Lord of Death, Timun, is anxious to meet me. But Ned insisted I stay."

Crackling reverberated in the tomb like a log on a campfire. Ned and Norbert stood, anticipating another obstacle. There was none. Sparks flew from the four torches. The flames flickered green and settled to a normal flame to relight the tomb.

"That was something," Tino said.

"Look! Labarre's ship is gone." Norbert pointed to the wall. "Like the water washed it away."

The waves, the sky, and even the small village in the distant land all remained. Just the ship had been washed off. Ned and Norbert shared a glance, but before either of them could say anything, the loud scraping of marble on marble interrupted them. The statue of Labarre slid back to reveal a faint blue light glowing from inside the sarcophagus.

Tino still hid in the doorway. "I'd stay away from it."

"What do you think?" Norbert asked.

"We've come this far. Seems fitting to finish." Ned walked toward the blue light.

Norbert followed him as Tino continued to protest from the door. Ned had expected Labarre's body to be grasping some sort of treasure, but the trick door hardly went deep enough into the sarcophagus. When Ned peered in, he saw a small cavity. He was thankful he didn't have to see Labarre's bones. Inside the small cavity were a rolled-up parchment and a brown leather sack. He grabbed both. The light faded. He held his breath, expecting another trap. Instead, the statue of Labarre slid shut to its original position.

The grinding of stone filled the tomb, and the statue of Goran moved again. Ned and Norbert stepped back, but the statue just pointed its trident at the door, and the torches extinguished.

Ned slid backward. "I think they're going to let us leave."

"No sense arguing with that." Norbert ran toward the door.

Ned followed him out of the tomb. As sunlight hit Ned's face, the stone door shut behind him. He and Norbert started laughing again.

"I see nothing funny about this," Tino said.

"Of course you don't." Norbert gave him a friendly push.

Tino rubbed his shoulder. "Why are you all wet?"

"What does the parchment say, Ned?" Norbert asked.

His heart in his throat, Ned slid it out of its leather case and unrolled it.

*Bear,*

*Cheers to surviving the journey that led you here. Only a truly remarkable bear could have made it to the remote island of Tortue. I wish I could have met you myself. The honor would have truly been mine.*

*Alas, I am not naive enough to think that my encouraging words were the only reward you desired. In my leather sack is a map to Goran's gold. I have seen this treasure, and it is far grander than one can comprehend.*

*The leather sack also contains the deed to your new ship, the Pelican. Take care of her as you would your ailing mother. There is magic in her planks, and she may deem you worthy enough to show you.*

*She has been washed from this tomb to the sea, and you shall find the instructions on how to retrieve her in the leather book. The book is the story of my final journey. I never got it back to the mainland. If you would be so kind as to deliver it to a shop in Wexlin, you will have my eternal gratitude. It's on the corner of Main and Harbor.*

*Heed my warning, bear. You and I are pieces in a game bigger than ourselves. You have been chosen by Goran, as I was chosen to lead you to him. The darkness of a godless time is over, and we are at their mercy.*

*Respectfully yours,*
*Ulrich Leon Labarre*

# Chapter 16
# The Harbor and the Tavern

Ned couldn't wait to see what else Labarre had left in the leather sack. Tino, Ivin, and Norbert crowded around him as he pulled out a scroll and a leather book. They all frowned. The scroll was wrapped in a gold seal with the stamp of a pelican. Ned tried to slide it off to see the deed of the ship, but the little pelican would not budge. He twisted and pulled, but the seal remained intact. He growled and threw it to the ground.

There had to be a way to get the seal off; he just needed to figure out how. He winced at what he had done and quickly retrieved the scroll. He examined the golden pelican more closely and ran his finger over the engraving. The seal vibrated. He held on as tightly as he could despite the pulsing bringing agony to his arm wound. He gritted his teeth and growled. The seal started to move, and to everyone's wonder, the engraving morphed into a golden pelican about the size of a hummingbird.

The tiny pelican spread its wings and stretched before flying off the scroll. It flapped its wings until it was eye level with Ned, where it soared in a big circle in front of him.

"It's incredible," Ivin said.

Ned's paws tingled. He felt like he could soar into the sky just like this little pelican. He reached out to catch it and put it back. The pelican darted away, flew ten yards to the east, and soared in a circle again. Ned followed. When he got within arm's reach, the pelican flew away from him and circled again.

"What are we going to do?" Tino asked.

"We're going to follow it." Ned packed up all his stuff.

Whenever one of them got close to the pelican, it flew away down a trail. They trotted along and tried to catch it until they realized they would be chasing it for a while. The golden pelican led them down the mountainside to the east of Tortue. Ned didn't feel nearly as tired while walking. He had a renewed energy after leaving Labarre's tomb.

"What do you think he meant by 'The darkness of a godless time is over'?" Norbert asked.

Ned flipped through Labarre's final book. "Not sure."

"You think we should give this whole thing up?" Ivin asked. "It's just he specifically warns you in the note."

"That you're at their mercy," Tino said. "Whose mercy? The gods? Or some pirate gang?"

"I don't know." Ned still searched through the book. He was trying to find the instructions Labarre had left him, but the journal wasn't well organized. "I'm going to see where this golden fella leads us, and then I'll decide what to do. Here it is." He held the small book closer to his face.

Tino stretched his neck up to see. "What does it say to do?"

"'The mountains in the east harbor are where my ship has washed to. As in a time of battle, you must declare what you are in order to retrieve your prize.'" Ned scratched the back of his neck. "That doesn't make sense."

"Good thing we have some time to think about it," Norbert said.

The journey from the top of the mountain to the east docks was a long one, so much so that the flying golden pelican became a novelty to them. They stopped trying to catch it and practically ignored it. Norbert, Tino, and Ivin had each taken turns asking Ned what he would do with the treasure or if they should even continue on after it. Ned didn't know if they were right or wrong. It didn't really matter, as he was going to do whatever Labarre had instructed him to do. Not out of loyalty or duty but sheer curiosity. It had been many years since Labarre had died. What would the condition of the ship be?

The newfound energy was sucked out of him. How was he going to fix a ship that had been left unattended for decades? Even if he knew how to do it, he'd need an entire crew's help to complete it in a timely manner.

Ned flexed his left paw to relieve the discomfort from his wound. He was starting to think this trip was going to be for nothing and that they were better off going to find the captain to help fix the *Ironwill*. The pain in his feet and legs informed him that stopping was the logical choice.

Through the thickness of the jungle, they came to a rocky clearing on the east side of the harbor. It was deserted, with a few small wooden docks running into the shallow waters. The sea cliffs, with little useable land, made the east part of the harbor utterly useless compared to the conditions of the west harbor. The golden pelican started to burn like a torch before it darted across the water and crashed into the cliffside.

Norbert eyed the small burning area where the pelican crashed. "Now what do we do?"

"What did the book say to do?" Ivin nudged Ned.

Tino stuck his head in the book. "It was useless."

As if a lightning bolt of information hit him, Ned figured out how to get Labarre's ship. Labarre knew only a bear could open his tomb. So only a bear could retrieve his instructions, and there was only one song all bears were guaranteed to know.

"I got it." Ned closed the book, catching the tip of Tino's nose.

"It's the war song. Here, hold this." He tossed the book to Tino, who rubbed his nose.

Ned walked alone onto one of the wooden docks and faced east to the tall sea cliffs as Labarre's note had instructed.

In the old tongue, he yelled to the east, "E-lo-hi A-ye-lv! A-ma Gi-gv!"

He repeated it several more times. It had been so long since he had sung the beginning of the bear war song he wasn't certain he had gotten it correct.

"E-lo-hi A-ye-lv! A-ma Gi-gv!"

Ned looked around, waiting for something to happen. His stomach sank as he retreated to the rocky shoreline where the others waited.

"What do those words mean?" Ivin asked.

"Earth, my body. Water, my blood." Ned kicked rocks out of his way. "I thought that's what Labarre meant when he said, 'As in a time of battle, you must declare what you are.' That's the opening to the bear war song. He had to know any bear who found his tomb would know that song."

"How do you know that?" Norbert asked.

"I told you, bears are only taught the one song, the war song. It's another clue that Labarre wanted a bear to have his ship."

"When do you bears sing this song?" Tino asked.

"We're supposed to say it before any formal combat."

"You didn't speak like that when you busted through the captain's door," Tino said.

"It's more of a ceremonial bear action these days."

Ned didn't want to think or talk about the bear war song. He wanted to know where that little bird went. It had led them down here to find the ship, so why didn't it work?

"Is there a dance that goes with the song?" Ivin asked.

"Do all the bears sing it together in a class at school?" Tino said.

A sharp wind forced Ned to close his eyes and made his nose

drip. In a matter of seconds, the cold breeze vanished. The temperature jumped up so fast, the sun seared his fur.

A loud crack echoed as the icy wind crashed into the rock and the cliffs began to crumble. The sea cliff split, and the rocks tumbled into the harbor, scattering the gulls. The sea cliffs revealed only darkness. The rocks stopped crumbling, yet there was still nothing there.

Lightning shot out of the sky and struck the darkness of the open sea cliffs. Ned exchanged glances with the others. *Is this really happening?* Three more bolts of lightning hit the same spot, and a fire roared above the water. Black smoke soared, nearly blocking out the sun. From the darkness, through the smoke and fire, the *Pelican,* her sails tightly wrapped, drifted into the empty east harbor.

The *Pelican* glided to the center of the harbor, the fire went out, and the sea cliffs closed back up. When they returned to form, they were not as tall as they had been before. Ned, Norbert, Tino, and Ivin all had their mouths open in astonishment. The infamous twenty-two-gun galleon was right in front of them, and it was theirs. The *Pelican* dropped her two anchors and bobbed slightly in small wakes. From what Ned could see, it looked like she was in impeccable condition. Or at the very least, she recently had all of her wood painted. Labarre had said the ship was magical, so that must be why she was still in great condition.

"Now what?" Tino said, out of breath.

Norbert held his belly. "We should eat."

"You're not going to explore the ship?" Ivin asked.

"We go find the captain," Ned said. "I don't know how to navigate this thing, and we'll need help guarding her and sailing her out of here. Besides, if there is anything funny on board, we could use some extra paws."

Ned couldn't wipe the smile from his face. He couldn't believe he owned a ship. It was the finest ship to have ever sailed and the only one to have sailed around the world, and he didn't know the first thing about how to sail it. That didn't matter. It was his.

"Tino, Ivin, see if you can stand guard. Norbert and I will bring back some food and hopefully the captain."

"I'm not going to be the first one on a ship that came out of the cliffs," Ivin said. "I'll stand guard on the shoreline."

"Me too," Tino said.

"Fine," Ned said. "We'll hurry back with supplies."

Ned and Norbert headed through the rocky terrain until it gradually transformed back into the tropical jungle.

"Mandrin is going to be happy to see us," Norbert said, a skip in his step. "You're going to sail with him, so you're about to make him an admiral. I imagine there should be some sort of ceremony. At the very least, I think we should buy him a new hat."

"We'll see if there is a hat store in town. You think we'll find enough of the crew?" Ned asked.

They continued through the jungle with talks of where they would sail the *Pelican* after they got Goran's gold and helped Mandrin take Wexlin. Norbert wanted to swim with the sea otters and dolphins in the great bay of Cuwar Island in the west. Ned desired to see the treeless cities of the Land of Only Man. They could go anywhere.

The city of Queen's Harbor was on the southern end of Tortue. The *Ironwill* had landed on the northern end where Ned had climbed up the mountain and came down the southern side.

Norbert ran to keep up with him. "When we get to the city, we will have walked the entire length of the island."

"I suppose you're right," Ned said. "Guess that means it's not a very big island."

"Or maybe you could slow down a bit. I've had to run most of it to keep up with you."

Ned gave him a sheepish grin. "Sorry. I'm just eager to get supplies and get back."

Ned slowed down so Norbert could catch his breath when they

reached the bustling beaches and the docks of the west harbor. It was far more crowded than Ned had anticipated, with nearly every creature from around the world barking and meowing in accents he had never heard. Even reptiles were welcome. Crocodiles and alligators basked in the sun on the sandy beaches.

The sand and wooden planks became cobbled roads. Between an inn and the cobbler hung the sign for the Lucky Thumb Tavern.

Norbert pointed at it. "We'll find some food in there."

Ned sniffed the air. The burnt smell of overcooked fish made him grimace. "I'm not sure we'll want to."

The Lucky Thumb Tavern was dimly lit by whale oil lamps on the outer walls. The creatures in the center of the room disappeared in the smoke and darkness. Ned could see well in the dark, especially all the glowing eyes that locked onto him. Silence fell.

He studied the room to let his eyes adjust to the new environment. To his left was a table of three pumas who were trembling, trying not to move. To his right was a table of five modestly dressed red wolves who bared their teeth, but they all slowly retreated to the wall. The table of crocodiles paid him no attention, as not even a bear would start a fight with more than two crocodiles. Once a crocodile got ahold of your paw with their teeth, you were going to lose that paw. The alligators, iguanas, and other lizards followed the crocodiles' lead and returned their attention to their own tables.

In front of him, a group of jaguars and ocelots rose to their feet and stood in defensive positions, their paws on the hilts of their swords or pistols. They backed away slowly and moved to flank him.

A raccoon in a plain tunic and a dirty black apron jumped up from behind the bar, aiming a large rifle at the cats. "You know the rules, cats! No weapons. And fighting is to be in the alley on agreeable terms."

"You going to let a bear in here?" a jaguar called from the back.

The raccoon turned to Ned, now aiming his rifle at him. "You got coin?"

"Yes."

"You here for drinking or trouble?" The raccoon peered down the sight of his gun.

"Tuna soup and cider."

Norbert tossed some coin on the counter. "Two soups and ciders."

The raccoon lowered the rifle and looked over at the pieces. "This won't cover it."

"It will more than cover it," Ned said. "Bring our ciders to that empty table in the back, and if your cider doesn't taste like dirt, I'll consider giving you more."

The raccoon put the silver in his pocket and aimed his rifle back over at the cats. "And for the likes of you. Have a seat, leave, or catch a bullet. Your choice."

Three of them stared at Ned, paws still on their swords. Ned unsheathed his claws.

"Have a seat, cats!" the raccoon yelled.

With a snarl, the jaguars slowly sat, eyes narrowed. Ned lowered his claws and took a seat at the empty table in the back of the tavern.

"That's that." The raccoon lowered his rifle. "Two ciders it is." He climbed back down behind the bar. He kept one paw on the rifle as he poured from the tap.

"Don't give me one of those raccoon-size mugs. I expect the biggest you've got," Ned said.

Ned scanned the patrons to find the captain or any member of the *Ironwill*. Most of the creatures had gone back to their business and paid no attention to him. He still thought it best to sit with his back up against the wall.

The raccoon brought over their drinks—a small raccoon-size mug for Norbert and a pitcher for Ned. Ned took a sip of the cider. It was warm and very dense with just the right amount of sour. He wouldn't describe it as good, but he had certainly tasted far worse. He handed the barkeep another piece of silver. The raccoon thanked him and scurried back behind the bar.

The tavern door swung open, bringing in a blinding light. The silhouette of the creature charged Ned. He couldn't make out who it was until she was near his table—Amina. He was happy to see her, although she didn't look happy to see them.

Growling, she pulled an empty chair from another table and sat across from Ned. "Where have you two been? You abandoned the captain."

"I didn't abandon him," Ned said.

"You did. Guidry and the damn otters ran him off his own ship. It was an armed mutiny. No vote. We were overrun by guns and blades. They would've never tried that with you on board or if Calico wasn't dead."

"I just went ashore to bury Pierre and—"

"A mutiny." Amina slammed her paw on the table. "I always knew Guidry hated us being on that ship."

"That's impossible," Norbert said. "How could they? With you, Jaja, and Kenson?"

"Jaja, Kenson, Nimbles, Luka, Vesna, the foxes, and even Felix Boucher stood with the captain. But there were too many guns, and the captain insisted we leave the *Ironwill* without bloodshed."

"Good luck to Guidry getting the ship fixed without Nimbles." Norbert snorted. "The *Ironwill* is more likely to rot in that bay where we left her than sail again."

"You find this funny, otter?" Amina snarled and narrowed her eyes at him like he was prey.

"Do you want me to answer that?" Norbert broke away from her gaze and sipped his mug nervously.

Amina slapped the mug out of his paws, spilling most of it on his dirty gray tunic. He said nothing and sat perfectly still, trying not to make eye contact with her.

"We're stranded on this island with no money, no supplies, and now no ship," she said.

Ned didn't make any sudden movements. "We have a ship."

Her eyes locked with his. "Where did you get a ship?"

"It's sort of a long story. I'm still trying to believe it myself, but, um, you know the *Pelican?*"

"Labarre's ship?" She tilted her head.

Ned fiddled with his drink and took a sip to soothe his dry throat. "Well, now it's my ship."

"Impossible."

"It's true." Norbert's voice cracked. "It's anchored in the east harbor."

"Who's guarding it?"

"Tino and Ivin," Ned said.

Amina rolled her eyes. "You idiots."

"We came here looking for the captain. Just needed food first," Ned said.

"I hope your ship is still there. The captain is with Jaja and the rest of them on the beach. He's been drinking his meals since the mutiny, so you're going to have to sober him up. Break camp, and meet me back at the ship. Felix, Big and Lil Eli, and I will go help guard it until you get there."

"Sure. Well, we're going to eat first," Ned said.

"I just slaughtered a hog on the beach. You can eat when you find the captain."

She stormed out of the tavern.

"My stomach is not going to like having pork two days in a row." Norbert rubbed his belly. "All that land meat gives me the... Anyway, we should go find the captain."

"Guidry took the *Ironwill.* I can't believe it," Ned said.

"He never liked that Mandrin took all those creatures in and made them officers. Always wanted us to be a river-otter-only ship. We should get going before Amina comes back." Norbert headed toward the exit.

## Ned Bear

Amina poked her head back in.

"We're leaving, Amina," Norbert said in the tone of a pup.

# Chapter 17
# The Pelican

Ned sighed at the endless sea of white tents on the beach. Some flew flags, but Mandrin would do nothing like that to draw attention to himself. Ned also wasn't keen on the possibility of having to poke his head inside any of these tents. If he wasn't careful, he could enter the wrong one and catch a sword or a bullet. Norbert followed as close as he could without riding on top of him.

Ned thought he saw the captain and pulled back the canvas to peer into the tent.

"Begone! I'm not food!" A ring-tailed cat in ripped black breeches darted underneath a wooden table.

"Sorry. Uh, wrong tent." Ned pulled his head back out.

"Try this one." Norbert pointed at a different tent up the trail. "I thought I saw Nimbles walk in there."

"You thought you saw, or you saw?" Ned asked.

Norbert blinked at him with wide eyes. "Yeah. I definitely saw him."

"You don't seem confident." Ned frowned. "Natty?" He stuck his head in.

"Why, ain't I a lucky cat," said a short, fat puma with frizzled fur that grew wildly around his neck and face. "I've always wanted to meet a bear. Sit. Tell me your story, or share a bottle of wine."

"Uh, no thanks. Have a good, um, day." Ned withdrew his head.

"Should've taken the bottle of wine," Norbert said.

Ned playfully pushed him, and they continued looking for the captain and the crew. He snorted and kicked the sand. His chest tightened while his stomach quivered. They were never going to find them. They were just wasting time. Why didn't Amina just tell them where he was? Ned dragged his feet and kicked up sand.

"Pfft. Watch it, Ned." Norbert spat out sand. "Hey, there he is!"

Jaja lay up against a log and poked at a dying fire. His elegant clothing was disheveled and covered in soot and dirt. His normal vibrant smile had been wiped from his face, and he stared through the embers.

"Jaja," Ned called to him.

He jumped up. "Ned? Where have you been?"

"I've come to see the captain."

The captain stumbled out of the tent with a full cup dripping in his paw. "One has to have a ship to be a captain." He finished his cup before hurling it in Ned's general direction, missing Ned and Norbert entirely. He continued with a slur in his voice. "No ship. No captain. We're stranded here. I told you I needed your help." He fell back into his tent.

"I told you we should've gotten him a hat." Norbert wiped drops of ale off his face. "He would've at least been happy to have a new hat."

"What will you do now, Ned?" Jaja asked.

Ned grinned. "I have a ship." He removed the leather parcel from his pack and handed it to Jaja.

The captain crept back out of his tent. "You stole a ship?"

"No, would've been hard with just the two of us, but we solved the Labarre riddle," Norbert said.

"The riddle? How? We're not even close to the ice island."

"It's quite the story. Gather your things, and we'll tell you about it on the way," Ned said.

"Bring the food," Norbert added.

* * *

Night had fallen as they made their way through the beach camps. Ned would have liked to stay and perhaps find a quieter place on the island. There was some real beauty in Tortue. Shaded white sand beaches with the warm blue ocean were what had likely drawn Labarre to this island.

Norbert and Jaja purchased food on their way through the camp while also discreetly asking about the whereabouts of the *Ironwill* and her crew. They had not seen the ship or any of its crew since they had been removed.

The sand turned into cobbled streets, then the jungle transformed into the rocky shores of the east harbor as Ned told them how he had acquired their new galleon. It wasn't until he told them about the sea cliffs opening to spit it out that Kenson groaned in disbelief.

When they joined the others, they stood in wonderment. The *Pelican*'s lanterns were lit, giving the ship a soft glow in the moonlight.

Tino and Ivin sat on the shoreline.

"Where are Amina and the others?" Ned asked.

"They swam out to guard the ship," Tino said.

Luka kicked off his boots. "I'll go get the boat."

Two dinghy boats lowered from the ship's starboard side.

Ivin pointed at them. "Looks like Amina can see us."

The boats drifted across the harbor toward the dock, each with a lantern in the front. They could not see who was rowing, and when the boats reached the docks, they were empty. Ned's stomach leapt.

"It's a ghost ship," Natty Nimbles said, his two large front teeth chattering.

"No." Tino stood tall with his shoulders back. "Labarre said the ship was magic. This is what he meant."

"You think we should just get into these boats and hope we aren't cursed." Vesna pushed the dinghy away from the dock, but it swayed back into position.

Mandrin looked up at him. "What do you think, Ned?"

"Labarre wanted someone to find his ship. I don't believe it's cursed." Ned scratched his jaw. "I say we go aboard and meet up with the others."

They climbed into the two boats. Most of them stepped in tentatively, expecting to fall into the hells of Timun. Once they were all seated, the boats glided over the water toward the *Pelican*.

The *Pelican*'s sides were stained black and varnished so thoroughly they shone in the moonlight. She had two painted patterns—green-and-white diagonal vertical stripes that ran from the bow to the stern on both sides. Under those stripes, a blue stripe with symmetric white triangles over it formed a pattern of blue-and-white triangles. On the bow was the wood carving of a large pelican with its wings extended as if it carried the ship on its back over the waves.

Ropes lowered from the deck, and they tied off the boats to be lifted out of the water. When they reached the deck, they saw that no one had been operating the pulleys. Amina, Felix, and the foxes were tied to the center mast. Amina scowled at them. Jaja, Mandrin, Luka, Vesna, Natty, and Kenson drew their weapons.

"How many are there?" Luka's voice bellowed even at a whisper.

"None." Amina sighed. "We swam aboard, and a rope—"

"A floating magic rope," Big Eli said.

Lil Eli grunted. "Dark magic."

"This is why Tino and I didn't go," Ivin said.

"I'll cut them loose." Luka stepped forward with his sword raised above his head.

He reached back, but a rope wrapped around his wrist and the hilt of the sword. He tried to wrestle his paw away, but the rope squeezed it like a giant snake until he dropped his sword. Before the metal had stopped bouncing on the deck, Luka was tied up on the center mast next to Big Eli.

"See! I told you. Magic rope," Big Eli said.

"What darkness is this ship?" Natty said to no one in particular. "I suggest we leave this place at once."

"Jaja agrees," Jaja said. "This ship will have us all."

Luka wrestled with his restraints despite Lil Eli telling him it was no use.

Ned tapped the deck. He glanced from bow to stern in search of help. *If the ship didn't want us here, she wouldn't have sent her two boats to come pick us up.*

In order to release the crew from their restraints, he decided he'd try the simplest solution.

"*Pelican,*" Ned yelled.

The ship's bell rang one time. The crew gasped.

"*Pelican,* thank you for securing the decks," Ned said. "But these are members of my crew. Please release them."

The bell toned once. The ropes fell to the whitewashed deck, freeing their occupants.

"Fascinating," Ned and Mandrin said in unison.

Ned's heart raced with excitement. It didn't matter that he didn't know anything about sailing, as he had a magic ship that listened to him. What else could he get the *Pelican* to do? He widened his eyes. What could the galleon do to him? His paws and feet tingled, and he flexed them to stop them from going numb.

What if the galleon decided she no longer wanted a bear for her captain? Blood pounded in his ears. They could be out in the middle of the ocean, and the ship could just throw them overboard and find a new crew. Could the ship sail on its own? And if it could, what if it decided to go somewhere Ned didn't want to go? His vision blurred, and he blinked rapidly to restore it.

"Ned, are you all right?" Tino asked.

"Yeah. Why?" Ned shook his head, thinking it would help.

Jaja put his hand on his shoulder. "Do you need to sit down, friend?"

"No." He shrugged off Jaja's hand. "Why are you all looking at me?"

His chest grew tight, his breathing shallow. He backed away from the crew. They were crowding him, and he was having a hard time breathing. His legs gave out, and he fell on his butt, panting.

"Get some fresh water!" Amina yelled.

Kenson and Jaja hurried to him and propped him up.

Ned gasped for air. "Thank you."

He caught his breath for a moment before having a feeling of weightlessness. His eyes rolled back, and he passed out.

*  *  *

Ned sprang up off the whitewashed deck. He was no longer out of breath, but his paws still trembled.

He climbed to his feet. "Why am I all wet?"

"Norbert threw water on you to try and wake you up." Natty cleaned his spectacles on his shirt. "How are you feeling?"

His neck and ears burned. "Embarrassed. What happened? How long have I been asleep?"

"I believe the burden of leadership on a ship you're at the mercy of hit you like a storm wave. You haven't been asleep long."

Ned frowned. It was true. He had been happy just to have found the ship, but he didn't truly understand what it took to be its captain. Especially with a magical ship he would never have full control over.

Natty patted his paw. "My father used to say, a creature who does not fear leadership is a creature too stupid to be in charge." He chuckled. "No one thinks any less of you. I'd be more concerned if none of this bothered you. You need anything?"

"No. I think I'm fine."

Natty smiled. "Good. Well, I'm going to get the others. You'll have few moments of joy as a captain, but the first day you get your ship is supposed to be one of them. Try and find some joy in today."

Ned nodded. "Thank you."

Ned inhaled deeply and took a moment to take it all in. The *Pelican* was a three-masted galleon that looked as fresh as if she had slid from the dry docks that morning. Her white sails were flawless and tied up perfectly with tightly woven rope. There were twenty-two cannons aboard the multideck ship. The decks looked freshly whitewashed and didn't bow beneath his weight. It hardly looked like a ship that had sailed around the known world.

"Gods be good, you're okay." Mandrin took his hat off. "My first commission as captain, I threw up for a week straight." He winked at Ned and grinned.

Norbert hugged Ned's leg. He wiped a tear from his eye. "Do you think she can sail on her own too?"

That was a good question. Ned was also grateful Norbert had changed the subject. He didn't want to talk about what had just happened. "*Pelican*, can you sail without a crew?"

The ship's bell rang once again.

"*Pelican*, should we hire more crew?"

The ship gave a dong instead of the familiar ring.

"Is that a no?"

The bell rang again.

"Fascinating." Mandrin stepped next to him. "*Pelican*, can you fire and load your own cannons?"

There was only the sound of distant gulls. Mandrin frowned and motioned for Ned to ask the question.

"*Pelican*, can you fire and load your own cannons?"

The ship responded with her familiar ring.

"Well then." Mandrin patted Ned on the back of the leg. "I believe there is no doubt the ship is yours."

No one could open the door to the captain's cabin except Ned. Nor would the ship permit anyone inside the cabin even when he asked her to. Inside the captain's cabin was a large, padded bed big enough for a bear. Red drapes hung from the walls, half open to let in light from the multiple windows. One wall was lined with fine walnut-stained cabinets with golden knobs. The other featured a tall wardrobe cabinet, a mirror fastened to the wall, and a series of rolled parchments and charts stacked on a shelf.

In the center, there was a carved table that flickered light to get Ned's attention. He approached it, and Labarre's world map appeared on its surface. The glow of the table moved in a rhythm like it was a reflection pool. He touched it. It was dry. A small ship ventured to several locations, and within mere seconds, it all vanished.

"You can navigate?" Ned asked the table.

Ink swirled on the table to spell out "Yes."

Ned widened his eyes. "I give you a map, and you know where to go?"

The table discharged ink like an octopus to form the word "Yes."

Ned's stomach leapt. He couldn't believe it. Labarre's ship—his ship—corresponded with him. And it was telling him he could go anywhere he wanted.

The ink moved around. "Captain, I have sensed the seal in your pack. As a formality, I must insist you present it to me at this time and place the paw of your injured arm flat on my surface."

Ned pulled out the deed to the ship. He placed it on the table and flattened it with his paws before setting his left paw flat on the table. The parchment melted as if the table had absorbed it. His heart raced. The table grabbed his paw. He tried to pull away, but it wouldn't budge. The wound on his arm burned and ached.

He growled. "What are you doing? Let go!"

Ink swirled. "I'm healing you."

Ned tried to slow his breathing, but the table's surface formed a goo that flowed up his arm to his elbow. He snarled and snorted at the liquid. It felt like it was going to burn his fur, then instantly turned as cold as ice. The goo receded down his healed forearm, returning his paw to him but not before pricking his fingertips.

He pulled his paw away to see a few drops of his blood before the table absorbed them. Black ink met gold ink, which then clashed with silver, making quite the spectacle as the trio danced across the table, intertwining and twisting until it was so tightly compacted together that it began to push the compressed liquid off the table.

A ring formed in the center. It was faded gold with the *Pelican* seal of Labarre. Now it was his *Pelican* seal. The golden pelican that led them to the harbor flew out of the table, circled around him, and finally rested on his ring. The ring entwined around the tiny bird, and his ring became the pelican.

Black swirls returned to speak to Ned once again. "Allow this ring to make our bond pure. Serve honestly with a good heart, and I will serve you true."

Ned slid the ring onto his left paw's ring claw. It fit perfectly. He looked it over with a satisfied smile. The ring made him want to stand taller and wear nicer clothes. He flexed his forearm. It felt so good after so many days of pain.

"You're a healer too?"

The ink twisted. "I can heal most wounds and ailments for you and for those you ask of me."

"Are you...?" Ned tried to think of the right word. "Alive?"

The black ink flowed thicker and moved more rapidly. "No. An enchanted object from an old spell. One not from your land's sorcerers. My loyalty is a gift, my third captain."

"Third? Who was your first captain? Who was this ship built for?"

The ink whirled longer than it had before. "A creature soiled in greed and driven mad by his own ambition. When I could, I chose Labarre."

"You can cast me out?"

"If you are no longer fit or endanger the crew, I will choose a more suitable captain."

Ned had never considered a mutiny from the ship was possible. "Will you warn me? Or will I just wake up in the ocean one night?"

"You will be warned."

"Can I trust you and my crew?"

"Yes. Their goals align with yours, and my goals are yours."

"Will you take us to Goran's gold and then help us lay siege to Wexlin?"

The black octopus ink shifted, then stopped, like it had wanted to write something and changed its mind. "Your fate is your own."

Ned grimaced. He spent most of the next hour asking the table about Labarre's travels and the travels ahead. He finally had the answers to some questions that had eluded him. Soon he had his journals and a quill on the table, where he filled in the gaps to his Labarre mysteries.

At the end of the world, there was a place where animals rode giant lizards into battle and even Labarre got to ride a mount when he visited. He learned of the barbarian monkeys that ruled over entire regions of jungles and kept humans as pets and slaves. Most importantly, it was revealed that Labarre had been under the guidance of Goran in an effort to bring a bear to him.

Ned scribbled in his journal. "Why didn't Labarre ever bring his own bear to Goran?"

"Maydia."

By sunset, Ned's quill had run out of ink. The ship had also shown him uncharted islands where Labarre had hidden gold and goods. It had never made sense why Labarre never brought back things he discovered or traded for in foreign lands. It was why so many creatures, including scholars, suspected his travels were nothing more than tall tales from a small river otter with big ambitions.

Ned leaned on the table. "*Pelican*, did Labarre steal you from the Land of Only Man?"

"Yes. My creator's path verged from mine. Labarre stowed away on this ship, and a partnership formed."

"Do you know how Labarre died?"

"He died alone on Tortue with only his sorceress to bury him. You are here to finish his life's mission."

The words washed away as if the ship knew the moment Ned had stopped reading. Pain pricked his heart. What a lonely way to die for a creature who impacted the lives of so many. Ned had always assumed he'd die in a field of mud and blood with his axes in his paws. The glorious death all bear generals promised their soldiers. An afterlife in the realm of Bojana where the streams were filled with endless salmon. Now he wanted nothing more than to grow old with those he loved around him.

"We depart for here immediately." The table showed a map of what Ned recognized as the Island of Winter. It zoomed in on a specific cove. "Your final quest begins here." Above the map, it spelled, "Here is the message Labarre asked I hold for you."

A bear-sized scroll emerged from the table and rolled toward Ned. He snatched it, his paws shaking. He unrolled it.

*Bear,*

*You must go on this journey alone as I did. I have left you clues to help you find your way and to better prepare yourself. Your first task will be to cross a swaying bridge. The bridge is meant to collapse. Your second task will be to climb up a waterfall. Third will be to navigate Goran's labyrinth. And your final task will be to defeat a god in combat. In my sketches below, I have included what you must do to overcome these challenges. Only then will all the riches and wonders in the world be yours. May luck and the gods favor you.*

*Truly,*

*Ulrich Leon Labarre*

Ned studied the four sketches. There was one of a bridge, a waterfall, a series of arrows pointing in various directions, and an upside-down sword. There were words, but he had a difficult time making out what they said. His legs felt weak, and he was light-headed. He fell into a small chair by the table. Even the thought of crossing the bridge sent a shiver down his spine. He was scared of walking on the wooden dock in Wexlin. How was he going to cross a swaying bridge that was supposed to collapse? Then climb up a waterfall? Only to make his way through a maze to fight a god?

His eyelids grew heavy as the last couple of days caught up with him. He wasn't sure if he was going to be able to do what Labarre wanted. He yawned. A rope pulled him away from the table and guided him toward his new bed.

He collapsed into the bed. Something pulled off his boots. The curtains closed themselves, blocking out the rising sun to put him in almost complete darkness. He closed his eyes, and within seconds, he was asleep.

**Chapter 18**
# The Island of Winter

The *Pelican* now allowed the crew into the captain's cabin with Ned's permission, and Ned showed them the table and the journey ahead. They leaned over the table and watched everything with wide eyes. There was no further debate, and they agreed to set out immediately. Kenson collected coin from everyone to purchase rations for the long journey to the Island of Winter and then back to Wexlin. The *Pelican* could do just about anything, but it could not create food from nothing.

After the *Pelican* lifted her own anchors, the crew had a difficult time adjusting to life on a magical sailing ship. Jaja stood by the wheel in case the ship needed him to steer. Kenson routinely checked the chart on the table with his own calculations to confirm the vessel remained on course. Amina still did her hourly inspections of the craft and the crew. Ivin and Tino handled the kitchen duties, while Luka, Vesna, and Norbert washed the already spotless decks.

Mandrin stood by Ned's side. Ned wanted to enjoy being a captain, but the dread of what was ahead of him lingered like a fly on a corpse. How was he going to defeat a god in combat? He was a capable fighter, but he would never describe himself as a good one.

"Maybe it's a riddle," Mandrin said. "Like everything else. Maybe you don't have to actually defeat a god. There could be another way."

"Reads straightforward to me." Ned tapped the railing. "I have to climb a waterfall and navigate a labyrinth before that becomes an issue. I think I'm making a mistake. I could get all of us killed."

Mandrin's eyebrows drew together, and he gave Ned a soft smile. "You could get us killed, but you could also be the one to save us and many more." He patted Ned's knee. "If you want to stop and turn around, we all will understand. I will fully support your decision. Your task would be difficult for just about any creature, but I'm confident that if there is a bear out there who could do this, it would be you."

Ned grimaced and looked away. "You don't even know me. I'm a deserter to my tribe and a terrible sailor. I don't know why I thought I could do this."

Mandrin grabbed his paw. "You're captain of the *Pelican*. The most famous ship the Land has ever known. On your own, you navigated the Northwest Forest, the Purple Mountains, the Great Plains, and the Muddy River. You unlocked a riddle scholars have been studying for decades, and you did it on a whim. Perhaps I don't know you as well as I should, but I'm a better otter for knowing you." He squeezed Ned's paw. "You have my support." He smiled and left Ned standing at the railing by himself.

Ned rubbed at the pain in his chest. He touched the golden pelican ring on his finger. Warmth coursed through his body, and the pain in his chest disappeared. If only he could show his mother and father that he had become a ship captain. Then maybe there would be less shame in his leaving.

As the *Pelican* sailed closer to the Island of Winter, the color of the ocean changed from a crisp aqua blue to nearly black. Ned stood on the deck as often as he could. A pod of whales seemed to be following them. Norbert called them blackfish, but Ned, like all northerners, knew them as orcas. They swam up to the side of the *Pelican* and stared at him.

A large male with a tall dorsal fin spent the most time following the ship. He appeared to be twice the size of the others and was heavily scarred. When he turned on his side to study Ned with his piercing black eye, the other orcas darted out of his way.

Ned stared back. It was as if each waited for the other to say something. When the whale had stared long enough, he vanished into the depths.

With everything on Ned's mind, he found the orcas to be a welcome distraction. The crew didn't agree. They all had heard the stories of how a pod of orcas would sink a ship for food. Fishers in the north often tossed a pod of orcas their best fish in hopes the whales would leave them be. This often worked unless the pod decided someone took too many fish or disrespected their territory in some way. If that was the case, there was no saving you.

"I'm glad we left the dolphins behind," Luka said every time the orcas swam up to the ship.

The *Pelican* made it to the Island of Winter after just three days at sea. Large cliffs of blue ice towered over the galleon, putting them in a shadowy darkness. A chill ran through Ned's fur and into his skin. He shuddered.

The crew was unprepared for the cold. Their supplies were aboard the *Ironwill*, and they had spent most of their coin on food. Following Jaja's lead, they wrapped themselves in the blankets from their beds and took refuge in the galley by the hearth. Vesna, Luka, and Ned were the only ones able to stay warm on deck, with occasional visits to the hearth in the captain's quarters.

The ice cliffs radiated a blue that glowed almost as brightly as the sorcerer's magic in Labarre's tomb. Ned spent a lot of time at the rail, hoping to catch a glimpse of the black flightless birds Labarre had loved so much from his book. He hadn't seen any the day the *Pelican* spent weaving in and out of the large snow-capped icebergs.

The *Pelican* tightened her mainsail, and the crew scrambled to their feet. That was a sure sign they were getting close to the mark on the map Labarre had made. The galleon rounded one last ice cliff, which made a cracking noise and dropped a large boulder of ice into the ocean. The ship bobbed in the wake as it rounded the bend.

As Labarre had described, a small tropical jungle sat in a canyon of ice. The jungle started at the top of the volcano and melted its way down to the bottom of the ice canyon. The canyon walls were smooth blue ice at the top that turned green from the reflecting jungle treetops. The jungle itself was like a road through the ice to a dormant volcano.

Ned retrieved the scroll Labarre had left for the journey to the entrance to Goran's lair.

The table flashed and glowed. "This quest you must complete on your own, Captain. Your crew will be needed elsewhere."

The words vanished, and another map with a clear trail appeared. Ned grabbed it and gave it a quick look-over. The trail went through the jungle to the base of the volcano where two swords had been drawn with the words *Final Test* written as a caption. He backtracked over the trail, running his claw along the dashed line. There were the same three tasks along the way. Labarre had left small notes on how to get by them.

Ned nearly dropped his map at the loud banging on his door.

"Captain." It was Norbert. "We're ready to depart for shore."

Ned left his cabin. The entire crew waited for him on the quarterdeck. He gave the map and Labarre's notes on the quest to Mandrin to examine.

"Labarre told me I'm to go alone," Ned said. "Maydia is likely still looking for us. I need you all ready to help the *Pelican* when he comes."

His words were met with grimaces and frowns.

"I don't care what Labarre says." Norbert crossed his arms. "I'm seeing this thing through to the end."

Jaja pulled his blanket tighter. "Won't you need us to carry the treasure back?"

"I thought so," Ned said. "But the *Pelican* told me when she gave me the map to the treasure that I'm to go alone. I don't like it any more than you. If you have an issue with it, take it up with the *Pelican*."

Mandrin handed him the map. "We shall wait here for your word. May good fortune shine on you so it may shine on us."

Norbert climbed into the dinghy with Ned. Before he had a chance to get settled, large ropes wrapped around him and pulled him onto the deck. The boat lowered into the water.

"Get these ropes off of me," Norbert said. "I helped with the tomb. I wanna go with Ned. Let go of me." He struggled against the ropes. "I give up. Just let go of me now. Feels like a bunch of snakes grabbing me, and it's disgusting."

The ropes released Norbert, and he shuddered.

Alone in the dinghy, Ned was shaking. He wanted to turn back, get on the ship, and return to Wexlin, but the boat continued to slosh through the icy waters. He closed his eyes and sighed. He took a deep breath to gather himself. There was no turning back.

The world fell into silence. There were no birds, no sound of the waves, and no sign of life. Just the boat sloshing toward the shore. He looked back at the *Pelican*. The crew stood at the rail, watching him. A sour feeling rushed through his stomach, and he fought the urge to vomit. His nerves started to set in when the dinghy beached itself on the rocky shore. He lost his battle against his nausea and unwillingly fed the arctic fish his lunch before climbing ashore.

# Chapter 19
# The Quest

The jungle was a mixture of pines and red maples that grew along the volcano, which were unlike the ferns and palms of Tortue. From the ship, it had appeared Ned was about to walk into a tropical jungle, and he didn't understand how that was possible with such a crisp chill in the air. This forest was similar to one on the coastal mountain he used to hibernate in. The familiarity of the flora helped calm his nerves.

He would've preferred to have some companionship, mostly for encouragement. He wasn't sure if he was going to survive this. How was he going to defeat a god in combat to get into the treasure room? Labarre failed to mention in his notes how it was possible to defeat an immortal. Even if he survived, did he really want to end the curse if that's what Maydia wanted? Would bringing back the magic be a good thing? All he wanted was the treasure, and he wasn't sure how he'd manage that even if he did find it. His mind trapped him.

With one step, he'd think bringing back the magic was good for everyone. Then he'd take another step and consider the possible horrors he could unleash. Gods and monsters who had been locked away for 187 years could unleash their wrath upon anyone they desired. Once he brought it all back, he would never be able to take it away again. He wished there was someone to tell him what to do.

His heart thumped, and he had trouble breathing. He never thought he would be in this position. He alone now had the chance, the power, to change the whole world, and he wasn't sure if he should or even if he was the right bear to make such a drastic decision. Mandrin only wanted the treasure, and Maydia only wanted to bring back the magic to find a sorcerer to reverse his curse. If it was something Maydia wanted, maybe it wasn't the right thing to do.

Roaring water interrupted his thoughts. The riverbed of rock had been carved smooth by the endless flow of the stream. The water was a sharp blue green with crashing white caps that plowed their way underneath the swaying bridge in front of him. He reviewed the map, remembering the bridge was the first note Labarre had written.

By the small drawing of the bridge, it said, "*One step, two step, three step, four skip. Repeat. Skip every fourth board.*"

It seemed simple enough. The bridge was made of ropes and boards that rocked in the gentle breeze. Ned stepped onto the first board, and it gave underneath his weight. He moved back onto solid ground, shivering in discomfort. He thought about the floating dock he had overcome to get on the *Ironwill* and how far he had come to get here. The difference was if he fell off this bridge, he would end up wherever this river stopped. If the fall didn't kill him first. His head spun, as did the world around him. He closed his eyes and took a deep breath. He had been able to conquer the dock when he was scared. He just needed to keep moving.

Ned stepped back onto the swaying bridge—one step. The board bowed. Step two. The bridge swayed. Step three. He'd have to skip the next board. He extended his left foot over the fourth board to the fifth. When his foot was secure, he hopped over the fourth board.

"That was easy."

Ned made it past the halfway point of the bridge with ease. "One step. Two step. Three step. Leap."

His foot slipped when it hit the icy board. He fell backward but caught himself on the handrail ropes. The bridge rocked and bounced, causing his heart to leap up into his throat and nearly out of his chest. He took another deep breath and waited for the bridge to stop moving. This only gave him the chance to notice how high up he was and how fast the rapids were below. He looked at his feet. He'd lost count of where he was supposed to step.

"One step. Two step. Three—"

The board fell out, sending his leg through the bridge. He held on to the arm ropes for his life as the river swallowed up the wooden plank. He pulled himself up, which caused the bridge to bounce and sway out of control. He stopped trying to count the boards and ran for the other side.

The wood from his missteps rained down into the river as he rushed across. His knees wobbled, so he never took his paws off the ropes. If his leg fell through, he pulled himself up and kept going. His body shook uncontrollably, and his lips quivered. *Just keep moving.* The solid ground grew closer, and he leapt for it. He landed with a thud, his head spinning.

He lay on the cold dirt and tried to catch his breath, his heart racing. His mouth felt like he had swallowed sand. Thankfully, he had brought a water sack.

It wasn't a long trek through the maple and pine forest till the trees gave way to a clearing settled under the shadows of a cliff. This was where he would find the second task. The water thundered twice as loud as before. A three-tier waterfall dominated the center of the rocks. Water rushed over the top, carving what looked like white stairs for a giant to walk up over the mountain.

Ned glanced over his map again. He somehow had to get behind the middle tier of the waterfall to find a cave. There was a trail that zig-zagged by the first tier of the waterfall. He had expected traps, but it had just been a steep walk instead. The mist from the waterfall seeped through his fur, and he shivered. He stood by the cold lagoon, staring up at the middle tier of the waterfall, looking for a path.

He hadn't expected to find an easy way up, but he also didn't anticipate having to scale the rocks behind the waterfall to the cave. After a long investigation, he found the jagged rocks behind the waterfall were the only way up. He took his time and slowly scaled up the slippery stones. The waterfall roared next to him, splashing him anytime he got close. The frigid water sent a chill into his bones. His mouth trembled. He had to press forward.

When he reached the midway point, his arms burned, and his knees shook. Not much farther up, the cliff began to bow behind the water where he had seen the cave.

The water hit him directly, trying to push him off his ledge. Ned fought with all his strength to move inch by inch up through the waterfall. His teeth chattered as the icy water cut through his fur. So much water ran over him that he could hardly see. He squinted and struggled to find his grips until he saw the ledge was within reach.

He started to rush. With what felt like his last bit of strength, he reached up through the rushing water to the ledge of the cave entrance. He dug both his claws in, but the strong waterfall pushed him down.

His claws scraped into the rock, and he kicked hopelessly for foot grips. He buried his claws in deeper and was able to stop himself from sliding. Now if he could only pull himself up. He tried but couldn't. All he could do was hang there. He searched for some sort of help—a foothold, a rope, anything—but there was nothing. He roared in desperation and kicked at the ledge, hoping to get some sort of grip, but his legs flailed aimlessly.

"I've made it too far for this!" His yell was muffled to a whisper by the waterfall.

He roared again and dug deep with every ounce of strength he had left. His arms shook as he started to pull himself up. He growled at his arms, hoping it would make them stronger. He just needed to get his chest to the ledge, but his grip wasn't firm enough on the slippery rock. Just as he was about to give up, something grabbed the scruff of his neck. He looked up and sucked in a breath. A sea otter?

"Do you want me to save you, or is this how you want to die?" the sea otter asked.

"Help me!"

With ease, the sea otter lifted Ned onto the ledge like he was a cub.

Ned lay on his back, energy depleted, trying to get the feeling back in his arms. His rescuer started to leave.

"Wait." Ned wiped the fur and water out of his eyes.

The sea otter poked his head out from the darkness of the cave. "You want me to wait for you?"

"Yeah. Why not?"

"I'm supposed to meet you at the end of the cave labyrinth. I really shouldn't be up here, to be honest." He frowned and rubbed his arm.

*I wonder if this is the god I'm supposed to fight.* "Oh. Can I walk with you?" *Hopefully I can find a weakness.* With how easily the sea otter had lifted him, Ned wasn't looking forward to the possibility of having to fight him.

"I don't know if you would want to." The otter tapped down his spear. "I'm supposed to kill you when you get to the gate." He smacked his lips as if killing Ned was an inconvenience.

Ned wrinkled his brow. He would have laughed if any other sea otter had said this to him. How could something so small be so strong? If that was what a sea otter god could do, what could one of the bigger and stronger gods do?

The sea otter wore dyed emerald-green sharkskin plated armor with a breastplate made of multiple layers and covering from his neck to his waist. His lower arms were shielded by vambraces that had sharp points at the elbows and were decorated with shark teeth. A skirt of layered sharkskin reached his knees, and greaves protected his legs.

Ned was armored with a small pack full of water and soaked scrolls.

He knew he should stand, but he simply lacked the strength to do so. He pushed himself into a sitting position. "What is your name, otter?"

"Right. I haven't introduced myself. I'm Duro, son of Goran. You are?"

"Ned, uh, Bear." His voice shook. *A god? How?* He leaned back and widened his eyes at Duro.

"No titles?"

"Oh, I guess I'd be Captain Ned. I own a ship." He had to scream to talk over the running water.

"What kind of ship?"

"A galleon. She's called the *Pelican*."

"Labarre's old ship?"

Ned's mouth fell open. "You knew Labarre?"

Duro scratched at a spot underneath his left vambrace. "I wouldn't say I knew him. He was the last one to visit here. He's just... It's a little bit of a walk to the gate. I'll tell you more on the way. I promise not to kill you until we get to the gate. Deal?"

"Uh, deal."

Duro walked down the cave and stopped to glance back. "No attacking me in the back on the way down there either."

Ned nodded, and Duro motioned for him to follow. The cave had smooth black walls and was large enough for Ned to walk upright. He was thankful Duro had found him because after three turns, he was certain he would have gotten lost in the labyrinth. When they were far enough away from the waterfall, darkness engulfed them.

"Hold up," Duro said. "You're going to like this."

Metal clanked against the ground. A piercing blue light nearly blinded Ned. He covered his eyes.

"Oh, sorry," Duro said. "Had it pointed the wrong way. All better."

Duro's spear had expanded into a three-pronged trident that lit the cave in front of them.

"How are you doing that?" Ned asked.

"God stone. You haven't seen one of these?"

"The ones that weren't destroyed were claimed by kings or other wealthy houses. None of them ever glowed." He must have been the first creature to see a working god stone in 150 winters. "You're one of the gods?"

"I'm one of the sons of Goran. But we are all given our duties. You know the saying, 'There's always a more powerful god.'"

Ned went to speak, but nothing came out. He didn't know what to think. He kept his distance from Duro, afraid the sea otter would turn on him and kill him. His body trembled as he nervously scratched his arm, trying to regain his composure, but it was no use. He was out of place and outmatched by this immortal.

"You haven't heard that before?" Duro asked. "I guess you wouldn't have. Nagi Tanka, the All Father as you creatures used to call him, is the one who tells us what to do. Things have been different since Bojana's curse. We're not permitted to mingle with the inferiors anymore. So talking with anyone who isn't my father is quite the treat for me."

They took a right at another split. Ned should have been paying more attention to where they were going, but he was walking with one of the immortals of the All Father. Legends from stories he had heard as a cub.

"I don't understand," Ned said. "There are a lot of creatures like you?"

"Of course. There is more to that giant palace on top of the Purple Mountains." Duro took the right tunnel. "Some of us are permitted to serve; others just got stuck down here when Bojana ended travel between the realms." He headed down the left tunnel at the next split. "You can't tell anyone that you spoke with me or that I saved your life." He snarled. "If you do, you'd better hope you're dead before I get to you."

Ned raised his eyebrows, then nodded. "Who am I going to tell? Besides, I'm going to be dead here soon anyway."

Duro put his paw on Ned's elbow. "You sick?"

"No. You said you were going to kill me."

"Oh, right. I had nearly forgotten about that. It's not much farther."

The cave never changed its shape. Smooth black walls and the same dirt path led to another fork in the road. Ned hung on Duro's every word. *What do I say to him?* The son of Goran, the god of the sea, walked with him, and Ned had so many questions that he was unsure where to begin. But he couldn't help but think he was heading to his own funeral. He didn't know whether he should be skipping along next to Duro or dragging his feet in fear of what came next. A wind whistled, echoing through the silence of the cave.

The deeper they got into the cave, the more bones of lost travelers appeared. There were all types of skeletons. Ned gasped at how many bear skulls lay scattered in the tunnel. He knew he was not the first bear to be here, but seeing their bones forced him to remember Pierre's warning. All the bears that came here before died. He wouldn't have been able to navigate this labyrinth, and if he really had to fight Duro, his bones would likely be added to the pile. He didn't even have a torch.

"What other abilities do you have?" Ned asked.

"Abilities? Only some of us receive godlike powers if we're worthy. Others rely on these stupid stones." He motioned to his trident. "I hope my father makes me the god of the sea after him. He keeps saying he wants to retire, that he doesn't want to work forever. But we'll see. My brother has been saying it's his role for over five hundred years now."

The blue light from the trident reflected off the golden gate just ahead.

"Do you think Goran will make your brother the new god of the sea over you?" Ned asked.

Duro shrugged. "He put Branimir in charge of all the fish. So he has his paws full already. My other brother, Vinko, watches over the tides and currents. My sister Hana nurtures all the sea plants. My youngest sister, Jasna, carries all the messages from Pa to the Purple Mountains. Pa calls her the messenger of the sea."

"And what did he put you in charge of?" Ned asked.

"He put me in charge of this gate because I'm the best fighter."

The gate was solid steel and had been plated with gold, which brought some elegance to the gloomy cave.

Duro used his stone to light the two torches that flanked the gate. "That's why I'm the guardian of the gate. You can see why I'd be the likely candidate to take over as god of the sea."

Duro hit the blunt end of his trident, and the stone stopped shining. He faced Ned with an intense look in his eyes. "You seem like a decent bear." He spun his trident over his head and got into a battle stance. "I'm sorry I have to kill you."

Ned had no choice but to prepare for battle. His arms were far too sore from climbing for a fight. Extending his claws somehow hurt his entire body. "Is there a way for me to get through that gate and for us to not have to fight? I don't even have a weapon."

Duro grinned. "You're going to love this part." He turned his back on Ned and retrieved a leather wrap.

He tossed it, and the wrap landed with a thud before unrolling itself. A bolt of lightning ran up Ned's spine. He couldn't believe it.

"The gods still have tricks." Duro laughed.

Ned's paws shook as he grabbed his two axes. He had tossed them into the sea before leaving for Wexlin, and now they were in his paws again. The wood and steel that once felt like an extension of his arms now felt awkward and heavy. Spinning them around again made his fur tingle.

"Are you going to tell me how you found these?" Ned ran his claw over where he had carved his initials into the handles. For years, these had been his only companions, the only things that kept him alive. He had abandoned them to leave that life behind, but they found their way back into his paws. It seemed he would never be able to be free of that life.

Duro resumed his battle stance. "In due time. Are you ready?"

Ned flipped the smaller axe into his right paw. He expected to have to parry more and worried about keeping the heavier axe up high. "As ready as I can be."

Duro charged, his trident locked on Ned.

Ned had been charged at before, so he wasn't worried. *Parry and spin. Parry and spin.*

Duro leapt high above Ned, the pommel of his weapon scraping the top of the cave.

*Uh oh.*

Ned jumped back, the trident skimming his foot. Before Ned could counter, Duro spun and brought his weapon down on him. Ned blocked it by crossing both axes. He hooked the staff and locked it in place, with the sharp prongs over his head. He clenched his jaw, straining from keeping the trident from hitting him.

"You've already made it further than the other bears." Duro smiled and tried to pull his weapon from Ned's grasp.

Ned wanted to pull the trident to the ground so he could step on it to disarm him, but the trident would not budge. Ned kicked Duro in the stomach, but he barely flinched. He laughed and returned a kick that sent Ned flying onto his tail. Ned wheezed and quickly struggled to his feet. Duro launched a barrage of stabbing attacks. Ned swatted them away. Steel clanked against steel.

His heel kicked the solid rock before the rest of his body fell against it. Ned's heart sank. Duro had backed him up against a wall. Ned roared.

"A roar? You're not going to beg? I really do hate that I have to kill you."

"I have no plans to die today."

Duro raised his eyebrow and chuckled. "If we would've met under different circumstances, I imagine we could've been friends." He shrugged. "It's nothing personal." He launched forward to deliver a final blow.

Ned hooked the trident away with his heavier axe, spun forward, and brought both axes down on Duro. He had practiced this defense before but never on an opponent so small. His blades swung over the ducking otter. Ned thrust his knee into Duro's head, which sent him stumbling back. Ned snarled.

"Nice move." Duro rubbed his jaw. "I thought I had you."

"The same." Ned winced. Fire shot up his knee when he walked on it. "You're lucky you're not a puma or a wolf. I'd be pulling this axe out of you."

Duro smirked. "I was really hoping I wasn't going to have to show you my best moves." He spun the trident around him. "Have you had enough?"

"Only if you're surrendering."

Duro snorted. "Hardly. You just seem like a decent bear. I'll let you in." He waved Ned over and went to open the gate.

Ned didn't move. *It's a trap.* His fur stood on end, and he raised his weapons. Duro waved him through again. *He just wants me to lower my guard.*

Duro rolled his eyes and leaned his trident up against the wall. "See? You have nothing to worry about."

Ned tilted his head. "You're just going to let me through?"

"Yeah. But if anyone asks, I easily defeated you and showed mercy. Deal?"

"Uh, deal. Why?"

"Bored. Been a while since I've had a visitor, and you seem nice. Not like all those other bears coming in here swinging. Want to see the barbute? That's why you're here, right?"

Ned cautiously followed Duro through the gate. He lowered

his weapons but not his guard. "Can I ask you why everyone thinks the barbute will end the curse?"

"Bojana abandoned her barbute, the source of her power." Duro shook his head and muttered to himself. "When you abandon the source of your power, you can cast a final spell or be granted a final wish. No one knows for certain what spell she cast, but whatever it was, it stopped travel between the realms and froze all magic for the mortals."

Duro pushed open a large wooden door. Light flooded out, causing Ned to squint.

"Figured you'd want to see this first."

Ned opened his eyes, and his jaw dropped. Tears filled his eyes and ran down his face. His legs wobbled, and he fell to his knees. His paws landed in gold coins that lay in piles all over the floor. He never thought he'd actually do it. He had found Goran's gold.

# Chapter 20
# The Cavern

Piles of gold and silver lay stacked as far as Ned could see. There were stockpiles of coins, bowls, jewelry, and whatever else held metal. Mounds of rubies, pearls, emeralds, sapphires, and gems of all colors. Rows of grand armor for all creatures lined the pathways around the towering piles of riches. His chest swelled with pride. He had been the one to find it. He thought about throwing the scrolls down, filling his sack with gold, and running out of there. He could feed all of Wexlin or any city with that much gold.

The reality of his situation hit him like the chill from the waterfall. He wasn't able to navigate the labyrinth without Duro, especially without a lantern. He was trapped in the treasure room and at Duro's mercy.

"Pa keeps all the magical artifacts, stones, and what he thinks is the important stuff in his private vault. It's underwater and guarded by the orcas. Little harder to get to. I've seen it, though."

"Really?"

"No. Not really." Duro frowned. "Pa doesn't let anyone go in there. Not even Branimir. His orcas are a mean bunch. Want to go see what new stuff the orcas brought?"

"Uh, sure."

Ned's breathing quickened, and he tightened his arms to his sides. He did his best to look casual as he followed Duro through the piles of riches. The standing armor lining the pathway held weapons at attention. Ned ducked under the spearheads of otter and beaver armor. The shiniest gold was separated from the dull or faded pieces. Gems had been removed from their jewelry, making for waves of colorful stacks. Piles of diamonds lay in the dirt like salt.

Tucked behind the piles was a tunnel guarded by two suits of gold-trimmed bear armor.

"Bear armor this far south?" Ned asked.

"Yep. From all over our territory. The orcas don't really care for this stuff to be in their ocean. If it's lost at sea, it comes here. That's how I found your axes."

Ned rubbed his thumbs across the hilts. "How did you know they were mine?"

Duro smiled. "The laws of deduction and my little secret." He winked, turned his back on Ned, and rummaged through a pile of leather. "Here we are."

He tossed Ned some leather straps. The metal buckles whipped him when he caught it. He winced, trying not to let Duro see how much it stung. The leather wasn't his, but for having been underwater, the straps and sheath were in great condition. Ned donned it and sheathed his axes on his back.

"This is seal leather, made by the ice bears." Ned adjusted one of the straps. "They bring it all the way down here?"

"Where else would they bring it? They're not going to give it back." Duro chuckled as they emerged into a large cavern.

The cavern was dull and lacked the elegance of the treasure room. There was a small, scattered pile of jewelry, dishes, and coins next to a large black pool. The pool was so still it added an eeriness to the water's dark surface. A large bubble interrupted the stillness until an orca fully emerged. The short dorsal fin told Ned it was female. She took a deep breath and spat a few gold coins to add to the modest pile.

"This is Lana. She belongs to the dominant pod in this area," Duro said.

The whale stared at Ned. It sent a shiver up his spine. She clicked and bellowed with her tongue, then disappeared into the black water.

"What was that?" Ned asked.

"I don't speak orca. They sort of just do their own thing."

"I thought Goran controlled them."

Duro laughed. "No. The orcas are the true rulers of the sea."

An orca surfaced. It was another female with a scarred dorsal fin. She tried to speak to Ned, then disappeared back underwater.

"That was Krita. Not sure what that was about. They typically don't just come here for a visit. Not an easy swim if they're not coming to drop off any treasure."

A familiar, heavily scarred male orca emerged, the same one who had followed Ned aboard the *Pelican*. The orca swam back and forth. He chirped and squeaked as the others had, but this time Ned heard a voice inside his head.

"Do you hear me?" the voice said.

Ned's mouth fell open, and his head spun. He rubbed his ears. Was he hearing voices?

"Did you do that?" Ned asked Duro.

"Do what?"

Ned looked back at the motionless orca. His mouth hung slightly open, his gaze on Ned. The orca chirped again.

"So you can hear me?" The voice in his head returned.

Ned peered down at the large orca. "Is that you?"

The orca nodded. "Call me Balo. You and I are bonded. Our legends speak of a bear rider. Never thought it would be me."

Ned swallowed hard as he fumbled for the right words. "What do you mean? What's happening?"

"Your ear can filter my language and I yours. By powers greater than us, I am your partner in the water, and you are my partner on land."

Ned blinked rapidly. "My partner?"

"Yes. You may call on me when needed. As I will call on you." He dove into the black water.

Ned's mind whirled, his muscles tingling. His heart raced. What had just happened?

Duro came up from behind. "Were you speaking to the orca?"

"Was I?"

"Only Pa has been able to do that. They won't even speak to Branimir. How'd you do that?"

"I don't know." Ned scratched his ear. "He just started talking, and I heard him but in my head. He said we were bonded partners."

Duro's jaw dropped. "I think that means you get to ride him. They're not like dolphins who let just about anyone ride them."

"What is the meaning of this?" a loud voice bellowed.

Duro turned toward a sea otter in elegant white robes. The sea otter's paws were clasped behind his back as he walked toward Ned. When he was close enough, Ned recognized him from Labarre's tomb. It was Goran. It had been Goran on the island who had led him and Ivin up the mountain. Ned's mouth fell open.

"How did you get in here, bear?" Goran asked.

Ned's fur tingled, and he scratched his forearm. Goran wasn't any bigger than other sea otters Ned had seen, but he carried himself with a confidence that made the hairs on the back of Ned's neck stand up. Ned tried to answer him, but the words got stuck in his throat.

"I brought him," Duro said.

"What? You brought him here?" Goran massaged his temples.

"Why would you do that? I gave you one simple job—don't let anyone past that gate."

"Pa, he was just hanging there." Duro put his head down. "I couldn't let him die."

Goran placed his hands on his hips. "That's exactly what you were supposed to do!"

"I thought I'd show him around a little bit." Duro, his head still down, kicked at a small rock.

"I don't want to hear anymore." Goran made a sweeping motion with his arms before turning his back on Duro and Ned.

"I was about to show him out, but the orca started talking to him."

"I don't care..." Goran froze and looked at Ned. His gaze softened. "The orca spoke to you?"

"Yeah. Said we were bonded," Ned said.

Goran rubbed his chin. "What did you come here for?"

Ned tried to swallow the lump in his throat. "The gold. Your treasure."

"Of course. But why? Why risk your life? For the wealth? Power?"

It had been none of those things for Ned. When he thought about it, he never truly believed they'd find it until he located the *Pelican*. Everything had always been about getting away. He thought about the night he had started the riot at the cathedral. The desperate, hungry horde begging for a meal while the jaguar priests got fat inside their golden towers.

"Started off just wanting to see more of the world, meet new creatures, write my own story. Then it became about survival. Not just for myself but for an entire city. I'm here to help them because I thought I was the only one who could. That gold isn't for me. It's to give an entire city a chance."

"By hiring an army to overthrow a ruler?" Goran crossed his arms.

"I don't see another way." Ned sighed. "Creatures are starving while those who are supposed to be looking after them turn a blind eye. We can't help them with what we have. We need power. And wealth is power. This was the only way I knew how to get it without ransacking towns."

Goran straightened. "Interesting."

Ned's finger burned. The ring from the *Pelican* glowed red and pulsed. He roared in pain and grabbed the ring. He tried to slide it off, but it seared whatever it touched.

"What is it?" Duro asked.

"The ring. It burns!" Ned held his paw.

Goran walked over to the dark pool. He knelt and stuck his paw underwater. He closed his eyes, took a deep breath, then turned to Ned. "Your ship is under attack. Four ships in the water. Seems your cause is all but lost." He dried his paw on his robes.

All the air was sucked out of Ned. He hadn't expected them to be attacked. Everyone was going to die, and it was all his fault. "Can you help me save my friends?" He fell to one knee as the room spun around him.

Goran waved his paw, and a helmet flew out of the black lagoon and into his paws. The helmet was completely smooth bronze with a nose bridge and eye slots designed for a bear.

Goran held it up. "You know what this is?" He wiped off the water with his robes. "Bojana's barbute. This alone is how you can save your friends."

Pierre's warning rang in Ned's head. *Don't put the barbute on. It's a trick.* He shook his head at the helmet and stumbled away from Goran. "I'm not worthy. I'll die."

"The barbute will decide your fate."

"No. It's a trick. Just help me get out of here so I can save them."

"You're not strong enough to save them. Nor could you reach them in time. This is the only way."

Unable to stop his paws from shaking, Ned accepted the helmet from Goran. This could be his last moment alive.

"But, Father—" Duro said.

Goran quieted him with a wave.

Ned ran his paw over the smooth sides. It looked like it would fit. Both sea otters stared at him. Ned swallowed hard. He had to do this. His crew needed him.

He slid the barbute onto his head. Everything went dark, then he collapsed.

# Chapter 21
# The Change

Ned opened and closed his eyes rapidly, trying to blink out the blurriness. He lay in shallow water somewhere different. The sky was a purple haze with a glowing violet sun peeking through lavender clouds. He stood, and the water leaving his fur to return to the shallows was the only sound he heard. When he walked forward, his feet slushed through the shin-deep water. He continued forward in no particular direction, sloshing along in the water until a mauve-colored fog overtook him.

His heart pounded. *Am I dead?* His knees buckled, and his whole body shook as if a cold wind bit through his fur. *Is this really the afterlife?* He stuck his paw in front of his face and could barely see it through the cloud. He pushed on. Water soaked through his breeches, making each step heavier. Through the fog, a small purple rock emerged on the horizon. He walked toward it.

The rock grew larger until it became a small hill. A smooth path cut through the jagged violet rocks and zig-zagged to the top of the hillside.

He had no idea how long he had been walking, but his legs ached like he had been for hours. He pushed on up the winding path of the narrowing hillside. As he climbed, all he could see were the vast shades of purple that made up the nothingness. The higher he hiked, the more he found the beauty in its simplicity. By the time he reached the top, a calmness had settled in his body that he had not felt in a long time.

Alone at the top was another bear in a simple white dress clasped at her shoulder. She stood with her paws behind her back, looking out over the vast landscape in the opposite direction. Her fur was mostly brown but highlighted with waves of black, and it shone like a newborn cub's. The closer he got to her, the more familiar she seemed.

Ned tilted his head. "Mother?"

The strange bear turned around. She was not his mother.

"I'm afraid not, Ned," she said in a soft voice.

"Am I dead?"

"Not yet."

"Am I dreaming?"

She shook her head.

"Should I be afraid?"

"Not of me. But of the burden you have chosen."

"What burden? The barbute? It didn't kill me?" A weight lifted off his shoulders like he had just placed a deer on the tanner's table after walking it back from a hunt.

She extended her paw to him. "I am Bojana, and I deem you, Ned, worthy to wear my barbute and possess my power."

Ned fell to his knees. How was this happening to him? In the songs, this sort of thing only happened to the sons of kings.

He shook his head, and his voice was choked with tears. "You're...you're... I'm not worthy. I didn't ask for this. I was just trying to save my friends and..."

She rubbed his shoulders. Ned looked into her eyes. They were calming and comforting, as if none of his problems existed anymore. Bojana smiled and embraced him as if he were her cub.

"Come. Let me show you something."

Bojana guided him to the ledge of the small hillside. They looked out over the vast landscape of purple mountains cascading up over the horizon.

"The land is odd, yet there is a simple beauty in it," Bojana said. "What am I to do with you, Ned? I offer you endless power, the power to bend the world as you deem fit. The ability to fight for the oppressed and the powerless. To give the voiceless a voice or a chance to take as much for yourself as you would like. This is the type of power most creatures spend their entire lives wishing for or seeking, and you deny me. Why? Is it fear? Or is your denial a mere charade?"

"I never wanted to be a fighter. I always found it meaningless." He looked at his paws, ashamed of the lives they had taken. "It could be fear. I fear now I will never be able to stop fighting."

"It's wise to understand the power you have been given. It's also a curse. This is why you alone are fit to carry this burden. So many bears look for the next fight, then there is you. A bear who leaves home rather than risk killing another bear. A bear who sought peace and found another fight." She caressed his face. "You will find your own path."

"Were you able to find yours?" Ned asked.

"I did. Instead of smothering the fire with a blanket, I built a straw city around it to try and contain the flames. We acted surprised when it all burned down. I see their faces when I sleep, all of them. I remember every one of them. I try to rationalize it to myself that it was for the betterment of the world. Wars... Rich creatures too ignorant or arrogant to solve their own issues. Instead, they make a game out of killing one another's poor. You can change it. You can change it all and give a voice to many who don't have one. Stop the kings and the nobility of the Land from their oppression. Rebalance power."

"I don't want that. I don't think I could do any of that. I thought I could use the barbute to save my friends and my ship." He lowered his head and wiped a tear from his cheek.

"You were here to steal gold to start a war to liberate a city, with the notion it is the right thing to do for the many. Governor Clayborn smothered his cathedral in gold while the otters of his city died of hunger." Bojana pushed Ned's chin up for him to look at her and took his face in her paws. "Doing the right thing for others is never easy. That's why most don't do it."

"Is it too late? Can you take the barbute away? Send me back?"

The idea of so much power terrified him. Like most young bears, he had dreamed of becoming like Bojana and the other gods from legend, but he also didn't know if he could trust himself. He always had someone telling him what to do, and when there was no one around, the rules of society with its armed guards were there to keep him and others in order. Would he always do the right thing when there was no one to tell him what to do?

Bojana studied his face. Ned feared she could read his thoughts until she pointed behind him.

Two paths lay before him. To the left were the mounds of jewels and piles of gold in Goran's treasure room. To the right was a small dirt trail that led to a large open field filled with colorful wildflowers.

"I offer you unlimited wealth. You can rebuild the world as you deem fit or lavishly spend all your days in comfort. Or I offer you eternal peace. You won't have any power or wealth, but you will be at peace with the world around you. Your only purpose will be to show others how to find the same comforts."

Ned couldn't shift his gaze from the piles of gemstones. "Which path can I take to stop Maydia from killing my friends?"

"That path is all that you dread. You will forever be burdened with my powers and my responsibilities. There is only one path to save your friends..." Bojana glanced over the cliff.

Ned looked over the ledge where the violet waves crashed into jagged amethyst rocks. "I'm supposed to climb down there?"

She shook her head. "Life is a leap into the unknown."

Ned gulped. He knew what he had to do, but he didn't want to believe it. Jumping off a cliff into a purple ocean on the advice of a god he thought was dead. But did he have another choice? He could take the first path back to the treasure room and be forever wealthy, but he'd be stranded there without the *Pelican*. He could always come back for the treasure, but someone needed to be alive to save Wexlin.

The second path was tempting. He left his home and came to Wexlin to find peace, and now Bojana was offering him exactly that. He wouldn't have to fight anymore. He could spend his days eating, drinking, and napping in a field of flowers. But he would be alone again. He was tempted by peace—the idea of never fighting again brought an ease over him—but he couldn't abandon his friends. After all, he was their captain now, and they would need him during the battle. He sighed. There really was only one choice. He took a deep breath.

"Wait." Bojana removed her necklace. "You will need this."

Ned took the necklace from her. It was a silver amulet of an owl with soaring wings and two small emeralds for eyes on a simple leather band.

"What is this?" He placed it around his neck.

"You will make many powerful enemies," Bojana said. "This will help you. It will neutralize and stop any and all magic. It prevents curses and spells from harming or stopping you or anyone who wears it. No magic will be able to hinder your free will."

Ned squeezed the amulet. Her words pierced him like a knife. He knew power invited power, but he hadn't had a chance to consider what types of enemies he would make. He swallowed and looked at the necklace again before nodding to her. He turned to jump over the cliff but stopped. There was something he had to ask.

"What was your actual wish before you tossed your barbute?"

"I wished for lasting peace." She smiled. "I hadn't foreseen all that came with that request."

Ned grinned. He hadn't expected something so simple. The way gods always spoke in the stories was poetic and like a song.

He took a few steps back and a deep breath. "Any words of wisdom before I go?"

"Find mercy when others see none. Be a symbol for peace, not destruction."

He nodded and thanked her one more time before he ran. When he reached the edge, he leapt as far as he could. His insides vibrated like they had the night he ran away from the army. He was excited for the unknown, yet lingering doubt squeezed his chest like a snake smothering him for its meal. He fell toward the violet waves. The wind whipped through his fur. He stuck his arms out like he was a soaring bird. He was approaching the water faster than he would've liked. He flailed and flapped his arms, trying to slow down. He screamed, but it was muted by the violet waves that engulfed him.

* * *

Ned sat up, gasping for air.

Duro cocked his head. "Oh, you're back."

He was back in the cave. "How long have I been out?"

"Not that long. Pa thought the barbute killed you. You feel different?"

He did. His body didn't ache anymore. He clutched the amulet. It hadn't been a dream. He had really met Bojana, and she had given him a gift. He squeezed the silver owl before holding it against his chest.

Ned stood and patted himself. It felt like his entire torso had grown larger and tighter. He flexed his arms in disbelief. His claws had grown larger, stronger, and sharper. Curious, he bent and jumped and nearly hit the ceiling of the tall cavern. He stumbled and fell to one knee when he landed. That had been higher than he had ever jumped before, and he did it with ease.

"I did it. It worked. It's finally over," Duro said. "I broke Bojana's curse by letting you in here."

Ned's ring glowed and burned. Only now he hardly felt it.

The still lagoon was disrupted by the large orca. "Come, Ned." Balo's voice rang in Ned's head. "I'll take you to your friends."

"I'm not going to be able to hold my breath that long," Ned said.

"The barbute will help you," Balo said. "Now get on."

Balo slid his body halfway out of the water and into the cavern. Ned finally got a real sense of how big Balo was. He was more than ten times larger than Ned, and his dorsal fin peaked at twice Ned's height. He cautiously approached Balo until he was close enough to place his paw on top of Balo's head. It was smooth and firm, exactly how he had imagined it would be.

"If you dig in with your claws, I'm going to leave you out there," Balo said.

"I'll never make it out there."

"You'll be fine. Do you want to save your ship?"

Ned's heart froze, then pounded, which sent a tingling throughout his body. He did his best to hide his smile, but he couldn't believe he was about to ride an orca. He thought it was something just to be pulled by dolphins, and now he was about to be a whale rider. He tried to swing his leg over Balo but failed.

"Just jump on. I can take the weight," Balo said.

Unsure, Ned jumped and slammed his face into Balo's back. After a mild struggle, he was able to sit up with a leg on each side of Balo. He held on to Balo's dorsal fin, and the massive whale swam backward into the lagoon. Ned expected the icy water to sting, but it was as soothing as a creek on a summer's day.

"Thank you for saving my life and then not killing me," Ned said to Duro.

Duro laughed. "Good luck with your ship. I hope our paths cross again someday."

They exchanged nods before Balo swam away.

"Hold your breath, and hang on." Balo plunged down into the darkness of the water.

Ned squeezed his legs as tightly as he could. Balo sped through the water. Ned closed his eyes to prevent the salt water from getting in. Balo darted through the darkness, and Ned slid from side to side on his back with each turn, tightening his grip on Balo's fin. Out of pure curiosity, Ned opened his eyes.

The water pressed into his eyes, and he could see underwater. He closed his eyes, shook his head, and reopened them. He laughed. He really could see underwater. The tunnels were like the ones he had walked through with Duro, only this time he glided through them on the back of a whale.

They had been swimming for a while, and Ned never felt like he was going to run out of air. He had been underwater longer than he had been in Labarre's tomb, but it seemed like he had just taken a deep breath. He chuckled, which left a small trail of air bubbles. He flattened his lips, remembering how close he had come to drowning before. The tunnels turned from a dreadful gray to a shimmering teal as they neared the surface.

Ned blew out some air, leaving bubbles to dance along the tunnel's ceiling. He stopped. His lungs still didn't hurt. It wasn't much longer before Balo surfaced.

"I can't believe how long I can hold my breath now." Ned wiped his fur out of his eyes.

"Told you you'd be fine," Balo said.

The echoing of cannon fire filled the air. Three ships fired on his. The *Pelican* was doing its best to avoid bombardment and return fire but with little success. One of the ships was the repaired *Ironwill*. Ned's blood boiled. He couldn't imagine how Mandrin felt at having his old crew trying to kill him. The second ship was the *Dirty Whisker*. He did not recognize the otter skull banner on the third ship, nor could he read the vessel's name. He growled and tightened his fist.

"What do you want to do?" Balo asked.

"Take me to the *Dirty Whisker*. We'll negotiate a cease-fire. Maydia just wants the curse to end and the treasure."

Balo blew air out of his blowhole. "That treasure belongs to us, the orcas, and he may not have it."

Ned closed his eyes, waiting for the mist to past. "I know. I was going to remind him of that. If he rejects it, I'll need another ride and some help. You and I just might be able to end this without having to kill anyone."

Ned squeezed his heels into Balo, and the whale dove back down out of sight. Ned closed his eyes and smiled. He was starting to enjoy being underwater. He found the water running through his fur and the quietness of the vast ocean to be soothing. He thought about Luka's and Vesna's faces when they saw him riding an orca, and he grinned from ear to ear.

They had gotten close enough to the ships that the sound of cannon fire thundered underwater.

Balo stopped. "I'm going to give you a push. The ship is right above us. Put your ankles and knees together, and stay steady."

Ned let go. Balo swam down, and Ned did as instructed. He put his legs together and floated in the emptiness of the ocean. Balo charged underneath him. Ned flinched. As kind as Balo had been to him, seeing him charge made Ned feel like his food. He now understood what it was like to be a salmon in a stream.

Balo's snout hit underneath Ned's feet, and he darted up like a geyser. Balo pushed him out over the waves. Ned flew above the ship's quarterdeck and leapt for it. He pushed off Balo in the air with ease and landed gracefully on the *Dirty Whisker*'s deck.

The deck rocked as the vessel unloaded another round of cannon fire. There was only one jaguar in mismatched armor on the quarterdeck.

"Hello again, Maydia."

Maydia faced him. "Ned, glad to see you survived. I must say, that helmet makes you look bigger and more bear than cub. Found the treasure, did you?"

"I did."

"My sincere gratitude, my dear bear."

Ned grunted.

Maydia smiled and approached. "What have they made you into, you poor bear?" He continued toward Ned. "Another spear for the gods? I was alive then. I saw the games the gods played. Used the stones to make armies fight one another. Towns were leveled and burned, but you think because you've found the barbute and were granted powers that we will all bend to your will. You forgot about everything else when you broke Bojana's curse."

Ned's jaw dropped. What did he do? Did he just unleash the wrath of the gods on the Land to save his friends? He tried swallowing but couldn't.

"So you do understand. You've allowed the gods and the magic back. More importantly, the god stones are also alive again." Maydia held up both paws to show Ned green leather gloves with a small glowing yellow stone in their palms.

"Gloves of Itlee, a jaguar god. A relic from long ago." Maydia adjusted the gloves. "If I recall, he claimed to be the god of music."

Maydia punched Ned in the snout. Thunder rang in Ned's head. His head spun as black spots danced in front of him. He fell back onto his tail. He grabbed the owl amulet, curious why it hadn't protected him from Maydia.

"They pack a bear-size punch, wouldn't you agree?" Maydia looked over his gloves. "Why would the god of music need such a destructive weapon? I've got plenty more of these little trinkets with stones on this ship. I've spent over two hundred years collecting them. No creature should have these powers. I see it as my duty to prevent these weapons from ever falling into the wrong paws. Starting with your new barbute."

# Chapter 22
# The Bargain

The *Dirty Whisker* bobbed and swayed as her decks shuddered from consistent cannon fire. Roberto Maydia stood tall over Ned, who had been knocked off his feet. The mismatched armor Maydia wore was encrusted with glowing jewels. Ned really didn't want to see what power those glowing stones gave Maydia, but it didn't look like he was going to have much of a choice.

Maydia reached behind his back to retrieve a rolled leather whip with a glowing red stone in the pommel. He unrolled its long tail, letting it fall to the deck. With a snap of his arm, the whip thundered and lit on fire. He motioned for Ned to stand.

Ned rose, shaking his head to clear his mind from the fog of Maydia's punch. Maydia had barely touched him, but it was the hardest Ned had ever been hit. Dizzy, he rapidly blinked until his sight fully returned. His heart pounded like the first time an axe had swung down on his shield in battle. He stood tall but stared at Maydia in disbelief.

Maydia stood across from him. "Ready, Ned?"

Ned slowly unsheathed one of his axes and took a step forward.

Maydia swung his whip over his head and brought it cracking down at him. Ned jumped back. The whip left a burning scorch mark on the deck.

Maydia unleashed a combination of snaps that Ned jumped, dodged, and rolled away from. He needed to find a way to get close and seize the whip. Usually, he'd try to catch it with his axe and pull Maydia in, but the whip would probably set him on fire.

With limited options, Ned threw pieces of the ship at Maydia—lanterns, railings, planks of wood ripped from the deck, bundles of rope, and the captain's cabin door. Maydia dodged or snapped his whip at the items, burning them or splitting them in half.

Ned ripped a chunk of wall off the captain's cabin and flung it at Maydia. Nothing stunned him. He roared and blindly hurled whatever he could. Through a hole in the captain's quarters, Ned saw four large water barrels. He grinned. He grabbed one, spun, and heaved it as hard as he could at Maydia. Maydia snapped it in half. It had not been filled with water like Ned thought. It was rum. The whip ignited the liquid, showering Maydia in an inferno wave that engulfed his armor and fur. Maydia screamed and frantically patted himself to smother the flames.

Ned froze at the wave of fire, but then his stomach leapt, reminding him he was in a fight. He didn't want to lose the only advantage he had. He threw another barrel, which struck Maydia in the chest and knocked him over the railing and onto the main deck. Fortunately for Maydia, this barrel was water and broke on top of him, extinguishing the flames. His crew stopped loading cannons or firing their weapons to come to his aid. Most of them had glowing weapons of their own. The fire had already spread onto the canvas, and Ned decided it was better to retreat than fight the entire crew. He grabbed Maydia's whip, sheathed his axe, and jumped into the ocean.

Balo and his pod waited nearby—a formidable force. There were countless black-and-white whales swimming around him, and despite being allies, it sent a shiver down Ned's spine to be at the mercy of so many.

Balo emerged in front of him. "You ready to sink some ships?"

Ned nodded. He grabbed Balo's dorsal fin and mounted him as he swam by. His paws tingled. He was already starting to get the hang of riding an orca. But he had to do something fast. Time was not on his side, and he had to reach his crew before Maydia unleashed those stones on them. Balo twisted and turned until he got the entire pod swimming toward the enemy ships.

"Six to a wedge, bulls to the back," Balo said. "Ready positions."

The others replied with chirps and clicks Ned didn't understand. His grip slipped on Balo's dorsal fin, and he slid back before catching himself. His heart leapt, as he had not expected Balo and the other whales to surface. He wiped water off his face, pushed the fur out of his eyes, and looked behind him. Well over fifty orcas lined up in rows in a wedge formation behind Balo.

"What are you doing?" Ned asked.

"Letting them see us. It's more dramatic." Balo laughed. "I'm joking. We need to be close to the surface to start the wake."

They headed toward the unknown ship on the *Dirty Whisker*'s right flank. It was a hickory-stained frigate with yellow trim and white sails. Her crew was a mixture of jaguars, ocelots, and other southern cats. Ned suspected they were another pirate ship docked in Tortue that was promised treasure from the *Ironwill* or Maydia. Ned couldn't see its name. It was the closest to the *Pelican* and struck his ship with tons of success. There didn't appear to be anyone on the deck of his ship, but he hoped they saw him coming. He took a deep breath, praying they were all hiding and that the worst hadn't happened.

"What about their cannons?" Ned asked.

As if the ship had heard him, cannon fire thundered, and steel balls flew across the sky.

Ned roared. "Look out!"

The cannonballs splashed into the water all around him. The

wedge had been disrupted, and there were gaps where there once were dorsal fins.

Ned tapped Balo. "They've been hit."

Balo swam along the surface. "Hold your positions."

Water splashed around Ned. Thunder roared from the frigate. Ned looked behind him, and the whales dove down out of sight in unison as cannonballs splashed in their wakes. They reemerged bunched together behind Balo.

Ned gasped. They were about to ram the port side. Balo swam under the frigate at an angle that created a massive wave. Row after row of whales dove down, causing waves to violently rock the ship back and forth until the final wedge of bigger males jumped out of the water and onto the side of the vessel to give the final push. The ship capsized and lay sideways in the freezing ocean water.

Balo circled back around. "Leave 'em or eat 'em, Ned?"

Ned almost gagged. "Leave them be."

"Fine. Jaguar is stringy and sour anyway. We can sink one other ship the same way. The bigger one you were on is going to be a problem."

"How many of your pod were hit?"

Balo swam around the pod while the whales regrouped. They all spoke to him, but Balo did not reply.

He sighed. "Two dead, six wounded. We didn't react to their first volley fast enough. Maybe we should've surfaced later, but I'm not sure we would have gotten the wake big enough."

Ned couldn't see Balo's face, but his tone indicated that Balo blamed himself. A heavy weight landed on Ned's shoulders and in his chest. He also felt responsible for the orcas' deaths. If it wasn't for him, none of them would be here.

Balo surfaced, and the other whales formed ranks behind him. The *Ironwill* tried to get the rest of her sails unfurled and out of the bay as fast as possible. On the quarterdeck, Guidry looked at him through a spyglass. It was hard to mistake him for anyone else, as there weren't many otters that plump. Ned waved. The otters swung on ropes and frantically ran around the decks. He'd seen the crew panic like this before, but this time it gave him a warm, fuzzy feeling.

"Shall we pursue?" Balo asked.

"No. Let them run," Ned said.

The *Ironwill* sailed out of the bay. Ned chuckled. He liked seeing Guidry cower away, but he found himself not wanting to harm the ship. Although it hadn't been the easiest of times, it still had been his home for a short while. He thought about all the meals he had cooked and the overall merriment of the crew before things turned for the worse. He thought they were his friends or were going to be his friends, but when things got bad, they were quick to blame him for their hardship. He recalled the days and nights he spent hiding in his cabin, how alone he was and how he cried himself to sleep.

He narrowed his eyes at the *Ironwill* when the ship finally steadied its course. He wasn't sure he'd ever forgive Guidry. He had cooked that otter's meals and sailed with him, and Guidry repaid him by joining their enemy, a jaguar whose crew murdered eight of his shipmates. All for petty revenge and greed. The *Ironwill*'s sails billowed, and it sailed fast enough to leave wakes of white water. Ned vowed to sink or take the *Ironwill* away from Guidry if he ever saw it again. *He doesn't deserve to be a captain.*

"Let them run? Are you sure? We could still sink them," Balo said.

"Yeah, I'm sure. We have a more pressing matter."

His ship was in serious trouble. The *Dirty Whisker* had tied itself to the *Pelican*, and the jaguars threw boards and other makeshift bridges to connect the two vessels. Jaguars swung from the *Dirty Whisker*'s rigging and landed on the deck of the *Pelican*. Warriors with glowing weapons swarmed over the planks. Ned needed to get back to his ship. His friends were going to be easily overrun and possibly killed. If they weren't dead already.

A single cannon thundered from the *Dirty Whisker*'s gun deck, followed by the cannonball splashing harmlessly over a hundred feet away from the pod. The whales stirred.

"Fishing formations!" Balo yelled.

The orcas scrambled away from the ship. They reorganized into smaller pods of four or five whales per group. Once they finished, they looped around, taking two wider flanks to circle the *Dirty Whisker*. They disguised their numbers by rotating who was on the surface.

Balo stayed on the surface with Ned on his back to not give away the ruse. The *Dirty Whisker* fired her cannons, but the whales were in too wide of a position. The *Dirty Whisker* only had swivel cannons on her bow and stern. Those cannons were smaller, and they were still too far away for those to reach them.

"How do you feel about another grand entrance?" Balo asked.

"Not particularly great." Ned wiped water off his face. He didn't know how he was going to stop any of those weapons with just his axes, but he had to try and save his friends.

"We're going to spin the ships. You disable the swivel cannons." Balo dove underwater.

The rest of the pods swam over to them. Small cannonballs from the swivel cannons sank harmlessly nearby. They were too deep for the cannonballs to reach them. The whales circled the *Dirty Whisker* and the *Pelican*. They were stacked ten whales tall in three groups with reserves nearby. In less than ten revolutions, the orcas got the ships to spin in a whirlpool. Ned's task seemed easier, seeing how well organized and disciplined the whales were. If they could effortlessly spin two ships, he could toss a couple cannons into the water. He didn't want to wait any longer. Every second that passed meant the difference between life and death for one of his friends.

"We need to get a little bit closer," Ned told Balo.

"Right. Just make sure you land on the *Dirty Whisker*."

When they were close enough, Balo jumped into the air with Ned standing on his back. They timed it perfectly for the *Dirty*

*Whisker* to spin into them. Ned leapt right into the cargo hold and crash-landed on barrels and supplies, splitting them open and spilling grain and salt all over the deck.

He tried to get to his feet but slipped on the grain and fell back down again. He adjusted his helmet and Maydia's whip that he slung over his shoulder. He bounded out of the cargo hold and onto the relatively empty main deck. Three soldiers leaned over the nearby railing and fed the fish their lunch. Ned did them a favor and pushed two of them over the railing. He grabbed the third by his shirt before he could draw his weapon and tossed him overboard.

The two swivel guns were left unguarded. He walked over to the small cannon and placed his paw in it. Still hot from just being fired. The cannon was mounted on flimsy wooden brackets. He didn't want to dull the blade of his axe and thought the bracket was thin enough that he could punch through it with or without his newfound strength. He glanced over his shoulder to make sure he wasn't about to be ambushed and punched through the support brackets. The cannon bounced off the railing and into the sea.

He checked his paw to see if he had cut it and smirked at his unharmed knuckles. He let out a small growl when he launched the other cannon into the sea. He had forgotten to check over his shoulder this time and was greeted by three jaguars and an ocelot with glowing spears and swords.

He had seen what the whip was capable of and didn't want to see what those weapons could do. He couldn't square off with all four of them, and there wasn't anything on the bow deck to throw. *Going to have to improvise this one.* He drew his axes and held them out wide before letting out a bellowing battle roar. The ocelot turned and ran, while the jaguars stood wide-eyed and still, their weapons shaking.

Ned charged, leapt, and crashed down onto the deck right in front of them. He growled and brought his axes down on a jaguar, who blocked him with his glowing red spear. The impact pushed

Ned's axes off the spear, and they vibrated in his paws. The jaguar dropped his weapon, which transformed back to a plain wooden handle with an iron blade. Ned kicked him in the chest and sent him through the railing and onto the main deck. He turned to block the sword one of the other jaguars was about to swing down on him. The yellow fire from the blade hissed as it burned the metal of Ned's smaller axe-head. He kicked out the jaguar's knees before the sword did any further damage to his axes.

He spun away from the jaguar on the ground to look for the other nearby soldier. A sharp pain sliced his belly. Fortunately, he had turned away in time for the spear to only graze him and leave a shallow cut. He dropped one of his axes, put his paw over his wound to stop the bleeding, and growled. The jaguar stabbed at him with a glowing green spear that Ned swatted away with his axe. Blood had stopped flowing over his claws, and he pulled his paw away to see that there was no cut.

He patted himself to see if he had been covering it, but there was no wound or pain. His newfound powers had healed him. He really had gained the strength of the immortals. The jaguar's mouth dropped open. Ned picked up his other axe, smiled, and shrugged. The jaguar slowly backed away.

"Enough!" a voice shouted from the main deck.

A large black jaguar in simple green plated leather armor waited for him. He had no glowing weapon, just a pistol pointed at the back of a bound and blindfolded Ivin. Lightning shot through Ned's body, and he tightened his grip on his axes and clenched his jaw.

"Enough. One more move, bear." He pressed the pistol into Ivin's neck.

Ned stood perfectly still on the spinning ship.

"Maydia will see you now." He motioned for Ned to go to the stern.

Ned extended his paw. "Give me the iguana."

"No." He gestured for Ned to follow.

Ned expected an ambush. There was a regiment of jaguars dressed in mismatched armor and holding glowing weapons, but they had pushed back and taken a defensive position on the stern. The black jaguar walked over to Maydia on the quarterdeck and threw Ivin to the ground with the other prisoners. Mandrin, Kenson, Amina, Jaja, Ivin, Nimbles, and Tino were bound and bloodied on their knees in front of Maydia. There was no Luka, Vesna, Big and Lil Eli, or Norbert. Where was Norbert? His heart pounded, and he gripped his axes even tighter.

"Surrender your weapons," Maydia said as Ned emerged in front of him. His fur was singed and his armor charred black. "You can put an end to all this madness."

The orcas' whirlpool still spun at top speed. Ned gritted his teeth. He wanted to run through them all to get to Maydia. He sheathed one of his axes and untied Maydia's whip from his shoulder. He let the whip fall to the deck, hoping it would ignite. He shook it. Nothing. He tried cracking it, but it only acted like a normal whip. He tapped on the red stone, trying to trigger the flames.

"You have no idea how to use that, do you?" Maydia asked. "The weapon chooses you, Ned. Give it to me before you hurt yourself."

"No. It still has some use to me. Besides, I'd rather hand it over to the orcas."

"I'll have no negotiations from you. Here are my terms." Maydia holstered his pistol. "In exchange for your life and the lives of your remaining crew members, I will gladly trade you for your ship, the gold you found, and Bojana's helmet. You must also stop the whales immediately."

"And we're getting?" Ned asked.

"You all get to live. You'll be our prisoners until we sell you, but what you do from there is up to you. A big, strong bear like yourself, I'm sure you could escape. Do we have an agreement?"

"You haven't really given me much of an option other than to fight it out."

"You're surrounded with no allies and just a couple of axes. You've been defeated. I'm empathetic in that regard. But my empathy does not extend my patience. Your barbute, or I start killing your friends."

Ned motioned to the ocean. "You forget I still have the whales."

"Can they fight on this deck?" Maydia smirked. "I admit they create an obstacle but one we will overcome."

Something moved over Maydia's shoulder. It was Norbert carrying two pistols. He was followed by Big and Lil Eli, Luka, and Vesna, all fully armed.

"Think it's time for better terms." Norbert aimed his pistols at Maydia.

The others also pointed their weapons at the jaguars holding the *Pelican*'s crew hostage.

"Hey, Ned." Norbert waved with a pistol.

"Interesting. Perhaps we can come to better terms." Maydia's leather gloves glowed yellow. "Or I'll keep the same terms. You all are soaked. I don't believe those pistols will fire."

Luka cocked his pistol. "Willing to bet your life on that?"

Ned froze. If Norbert was bluffing, they'd likely all die. If he wasn't, it would be easier to negotiate terms where they could leave. The tension of the standoff hung in the air. What would Bojana have told him to do? Her words rang in his head: *Find mercy when others see none.*

"That's it," Ned said, getting everybody's attention. "Maydia, I offer you a peaceful resolution. Lower your weapons."

Ned removed his helmet and threw Maydia's whip to the closest jaguar. He unsheathed his axes and tossed them on the deck, close enough to him if things went sour. Reluctantly, Norbert lowered his pistol and placed it on the deck in front of him. Maydia glanced around before sighing and setting his weapon on the deck nearby. One by one, everyone followed Ned's lead.

"You have our attention, Ned." Maydia stepped toward the

prisoners. He reminded Ned he was still a threat by showing him the glowing stones on his paws before crossing his arms.

"Having been alive before the gods' war and the Great Purge, you're familiar with *Bojana's Articles of War*?" Ned asked.

"What does that have to do with anything?" the black jaguar yelled.

Maydia waved his paw. "I have read it. It's been some years since I've seen it."

"Article two states that in war there is no good versus evil. There is good and evil on both sides. There never is a side of pure evil or pure good. Only different perspectives on a mutual conflict."

Maydia nodded. "I remember. She also states in article six that to remain neutral is to side with evil. So where does that put us?"

"It would be fair to say our conflict is our lives and the treasure?"

Maydia nodded again.

"The treasure is not mine to bargain. Although I have found it, I have not been granted permission to it. For the treasure, you may bargain with the orcas or navigate the labyrinth yourself."

Still circling the two ships, Balo sprayed water out of his blowhole loudly in agreement. The rest of the pod followed his lead until there was a symphony of spraying water.

Maydia looked at the black jaguar next to him. "How can we trust what you're saying is true?"

"You've searched my ship."

"We tried. Your ship still has some of my crew tied up over there."

"Upon their release, you and I will walk every inch of my decks together until you are satisfied. Can we consider for these talks that you were satisfied after searching my ship and that the treasure is not yours or mine?"

The black jaguar next to Maydia raised his eyebrows.

Maydia frowned at him. "We agree the treasure is not either of ours to bargain over."

"As for all of our lives, my crew will return to our ship. Your crew will remain here. Each ship will sail its separate way."

"No deal." Maydia removed a pistol from behind his back and pointed it at Mandrin. "I prefer to take our chances without having to worry about you sticking your nose in our business."

Ned stepped forward, and every spear on the ship was pointed at him. He clutched the owl amulet around his neck. "Wait!" He held up a paw to stop Maydia. "I can offer you and your crew your freedom."

"How?" Maydia cocked his head. "I don't understand."

Ned held up the amulet for everyone to see. "Bojana's amulet. It will cure any magical curse. By nightfall, you all will be healed."

"How do I know this isn't some sort of trick?" Maydia crossed his arms. "Just a way to get us to lower our guard to save your friends."

"Would you prefer we fight to see who gets to leave? Your crew has been at sea a long time, Captain. We're not enemies. You were merely pursuing us for your freedom, which I will give to you. Therefore, our conflict should be resolved."

"What guarantee do we have that this trinket of yours will work? Or that your ship won't fire upon us as we're leaving?"

"I'll remain on your ship until you're out of range of the *Pelican*."

Maydia looked around the ship one more time. He started untying the *Pelican* crew members. The black jaguar protested, but Maydia silenced him. When they were all loose, he ushered them toward Ned.

"I agree to your terms with one further amendment."

Ned stood at attention and took a few steps toward him.

"You will have a cup of the rum you threw at me and tell me about what all that treasure looked like. It is the least you can do for this..." Maydia gestured at his burnt fur and armor.

Ned smirked. "I agree to your terms."

Both crews erupted in cheers.

# Chapter 23
# The Journal

A chorus of screeching sea birds echoed in the stale air. The *Pelican* nestled in the bay, with the green pine forest as her backdrop. She hardly looked battle-scarred from the decks of the *Dirty Whisker*. After all the chaos that had just occurred in the bay, Ned's ship floated peacefully in the still water. Standing beside Maydia, Ned wanted to take in this place's beauty for all its wonder. He was likely never to return here and wanted to remember as much about it as he could.

On top of the fifty-foot cliffs, he saw the little round birds Labarre had described. They had flippers instead of wings and waddled when they walked. Ned smiled. He was happy he got to see the birds Labarre had admired and had written so much about.

A jaguar warrior approached Maydia and Ned. He gave Maydia Ned's owl amulet and bowed his head.

"Everyone is healed?" Maydia asked.

"Yes, my lord." The warrior bowed again and walked away.

Maydia stared at the amulet. He spun it before placing it around his neck. His body shook, and his fur glowed in the sunlight before a small ball of light drifted from the amulet and floated away. He gasped for air like he had just run up a hill. He looked over his body.

"I...I can feel." Maydia gave a small chuckle, a tear in his eye. "I didn't think it would actually work." He lifted his leg and moved his foot around. "I can really feel everything again." He fell onto the railing, having to hold himself up. "I've forgotten what it's like to be sore from battle." He laughed again before removing the amulet. He stared at it a while longer before giving it back to Ned. "Thank you."

Ned placed it around his neck. "What will you do now?"

"I don't know." He gave Ned a half smile. "I laughed when the sorcerers cursed us. I suppose I thought we could reverse it someday. Find another sorcerer willing to do our bidding when we wanted to leave the sea. I called them fools for making *me* immortal even if I was bound to the sea. With immortality comes power. But as time went on, the sorcerers and wizards grew old and died. And then one day there were none."

He rubbed his face. "Years passed, and I swore revenge. Revenge on the gods, on my emperor, on my commanding officers, on magic itself, and on every single jaguar who had ever wronged me." He shook his head and sighed. "How many lifetimes would that have taken me? Time had already rid me of most of them. I wasted so many years plotting, hating the world and then myself."

Ned took a step closer to him. He considered patting him on the back, but he hesitated. He couldn't comfort him. This was the jaguar who ordered the death of his friends. He had tried to keelhaul Mandrin, had Calico shot after he won a fair duel, and had ordered the rifle fire that killed Pierre. He couldn't overlook the pain Maydia had caused him.

"Do you have any family?" Ned asked.

Maydia paused, his eyes misting. "I had a son. I'd requested a transfer of duties so I could have been home with him while he was a cub. My commanding officer granted the transfer on the condition I finish my scheduled trade run to Tortue first. But I never made it back to land. I watched him grow old from my ship. When the news of his death reached me...I went mad."

Ned thought about what he might've done in Maydia's situation. If he had a son taken away from him or even his mother, would he have been able to remain rational? Or like Maydia, would he have scoured the world for a solution? Ned frowned, as he knew the answer. He placed his paw on Maydia's shoulder, his anger momentarily lapsing. Maydia flinched, likely not used to sympathetic gestures from a foe. He looked up at Ned, and his shoulders relaxed.

"Others would have done the same in your situation." Ned sighed. "I can't forgive you for what you've done, but I can understand why you did it."

Maydia nodded. "What am I to you? Ally? Enemy?"

Ned smirked. "I'm hoping you're retired."

Maydia laughed. "I have grand cubs with grand cubs of their own now. I'd like to sit in my keep and listen to stories about my son and the family I never knew."

"That sounds nice." Ned envisioned returning to his own family one day. He wanted to hug his parents. To tell them he wasn't a deserter. That he was a ship captain and an explorer. He wanted to amuse them with tales of his adventures. But Maydia wasn't like him and wouldn't find peace in that. He knew bears like Maydia. Maydia wouldn't stay idle long. "But I know you won't be able to do that forever."

Maydia caressed the yellow stone in the green gloves, the ones he'd hit Ned with earlier. He tucked them into his belt. "I've collected as many of these stones as I could from the sea. Some we used, some we destroyed, and the others I had buried on a remote island, the exact location unknown to me. I have them guarded to keep them out of not just the wrong paws but all paws. A new world is coming. I can't let these stones rule us again. When the time comes—"

"Rest first, Roberto. You have sailed too long and have much catching up to do. When the time comes, know that I have no interest in seeing these stones spin us into chaos as they have done before."

Maydia extended his paw. "You're a good bear, Ned. I wish our paths had crossed under different circumstances."

Ned slid his paw over Maydia's. "Thank you. Perhaps our paths will cross again but on the same side of the river."

They nodded to each other one last time. Ned jumped into the ocean for Balo to pick him up. The giant pod of orcas escorted the ship out of the bay and then dispersed, leaving Balo and Ned alone on their way back to the *Pelican*.

"Heading back?" Balo asked.

"Yeah. Liberate Wexlin. Bojana seemed to think it was the right thing to do."

"But that's not what you want to do?"

"I don't know if it's about what I want anymore." Ned looked over the bronze barbute. "Will you follow us?"

"My father used to tell me about when he was a calf and how his father had patrolled before Bojana's curse. I'm afraid protecting the ocean will become more challenging. Gods will be fighting gods. Stones giving powers to those who don't fully understand them. The world will be complicated. My pod will stay close by, but my duties to the ocean are my first priority."

"Understood."

Balo closed in on the *Pelican*. "How'd you know Maydia would listen to your offer?"

"I didn't see any other way."

"The god of war making bargains." Balo laughed.

"Bojana was never the god of war. That was always a common misconception. She was the goddess of battle strategy and warfare. Along with wisdom, intelligence, skill, and reason. Most importantly, she was the goddess of peace."

Ned frowned. He would have never used any of those qualities to describe himself. Wisdom? Intelligence? What made him think he could do this? That he was the right bear to carry on Bojana's legacy?

Balo swam alongside the *Pelican*.

Ned twirled the barbute in his paws before placing it on Balo's back. "Find a safe place to hide this." He climbed off Balo and onto the *Pelican*.

"No." Balo dove to retrieve the barbute and spat it back at Ned, who caught it. "Bojana chose you. It's your duty to her to keep it."

"I'm not sure I'm the right bear for the job. I'll never be like Bojana. I suppose I'm afraid I'm never going to be wise enough."

"You don't have to be wise or be like Bojana to wear that helmet. Orcas have an old saying, 'The calf never swims behind the father.' Make your own path, Ned. You will never be her, so there is no sense in trying."

Ned put the wet helmet on his head. "Thank you, Balo."

"Good luck. Until our paths cross again."

Balo spat water at Ned, soaking him, before he dove out of sight. Ned laughed and climbed up the cargo net. On the main deck, he was greeted by the entire crew, his friends. They embraced him and thanked him for saving their lives. His body shook until he burst into a fit of laughter that pushed tears out of the corners of his eyes. He had been alone so long. To have so many friends was a real joy. Finally, he wasn't alone anymore.

"I'm sorry we didn't get the gold, Captain," Ned said.

"Call me Elick. You're the captain, Ned. And we'll find another way."

Jaja patted Ned on the back. "Where to now, Captain Ned?"

"Someplace warm, please," Norbert said.

"Resupply in Tortue, then back to Wexlin?" Ned asked.

They all nodded. A loud bang from the opposite side of the deck caused them all to flinch.

"Sorry. They slipped." Duro's wet clothing stuck to his body, four large sacks overflowing with coins and gems at his feet. "This ought to be enough."

"Ned, who is this?" Norbert's jaw hung open. "Is all that real? Are those real emeralds?"

"Yes. They're very real. Duro, son of Goran," Duro said. "Nice to meet you all."

Duro made his way around the crew and slid his paw pad over all of theirs. Eyes wide and bodies stiff, the crew stared at him as he greeted everyone with a smile and merriment.

"Duro, what is all of this?" Ned pointed at the pile of coins.

"Oh, Pa said I needed to leave. Bojana had me trapped in there. Now she doesn't. So I thought I'd see the world a bit. I'm coming with you. Brought the gold for your castle battle and as payment to be part of the crew. I could use a good fight. Been a long time since I got to use my trident in the water. Only with your approval, of course."

Ned glanced at the rest of his friends. They all seemed frozen in place with their mouths open or a flat gaze fixed on Duro. No one said no.

"As long as you understand you don't hold a higher rank than anyone else here. We're all equal. Welcome aboard, Duro," Ned said.

Duro pumped his fist. "The dolphins have the rest of my things and a couple more sacks of gold. Which one of you is going to go...? Never mind. Same rank. I'll go get them."

"You have dolphins?" Luka asked.

"Of course. A whole pod of them. I call them hourglass dolphins because they have white hourglasses on their sides."

"I'm sure there has to be a better name for them than that," Vesna said.

"Nope. That's what I call them. Come on. I'll show you."

"I thought you had an orca," Luka said.

Duro laughed. "An orca? I wish. I've tried, but no one has one. Except for my father and Ned."

"Ned, how did you get that orca to let you ride him?" Luka asked.

Ned grinned. "Duro will tell you about it." He headed to his cabin.

"I sure will." Duro put his arms around Luka and Vesna. "I saw the whole thing from the top of the volcano..."

Ned took refuge to dry off and warm himself in his cabin. Norbert followed.

Ned pulled a chair up to the table. "How did the group of you escape Maydia?"

Norbert frowned. "One of them knocked Jaja through a wall, and we jumped ship. Didn't know about the orcas." He chuckled while polishing Pierre's lute. "They pushed us out of the whirlpool with their snouts. I screamed, thinking I was getting eaten. I thought I was a goner. Horrible way to die. I may never eat a live fish again. I only stopped screaming when she swam away."

Ned laughed. "I know the feeling. My whale made me feel like a salmon in a shallow stream." He smiled. "*Pelican*, pull anchor, and set a course for Tortue."

The ship's bell rang, followed by the clicking of the anchor chain.

Norbert sat on a pillow on the floor and played with the lute's strings. He struggled initially until he found his bearings. The tune was soft and carried a soothing rhythm. He closed his eyes and swayed to his music. He abruptly stopped.

"Sorry," Norbert said. "I got lost in it."

"It was great. I didn't know you knew how to play," Ned said.

"I was the one who taught Pierre. I gave him this lute. He sure loved to play."

Norbert sniffed, then continued playing as Ned listened. Pierre was the only other person he had heard play music, and he thought they both played wonderfully. His mind drifted to thoughts of Pierre. He wished he was here to share their victory. He wanted nothing more than to hear his voice again, to hear him sing. Ned closed his eyes and took a deep breath, remembering the day when Pierre sang him "Master of the Sea." Pierre would have loved to have sung it to Goran or Duro. Ned held his amulet. It had quickly become a coping habit for him.

He sighed and took out his leather pack and placed all his books on the table. He put all of Labarre's books in one stack, the loose-leaf papers and scrolls he had gotten from Mama in a pile, and his journals in another neat stack. He stared at them. His entire journey and now new life had started with these seemingly worthless piles of parchment.

He grabbed the book he had retrieved from Labarre's tomb. He had been so tired from the battle but had found a new burst of energy to read a Labarre quest that no other creature had read. He studied the cover. It was simple brown leather, and the pages were written in Labarre's own scratches. Ned put it down.

He eyed the third pile of books and his thin journal of stories from when he left home. Stories he saw as silly in comparison to Labarre's. He tossed the unread Labarre book aside and picked up the journal he had started for this sea journey. He had not written in it since the day they set sail.

Ned grabbed some ink and a quill and opened the journal to the first empty page and scribbled, *The Bear Who Rode an Orca.* He smiled.

Now he could write his own stories.

# Our Ned Bear

# Acknowledgments

Although Ned's story is clearly a work of fiction, there is a layer of truth to who Ned is. Ned's character is based on my Siberian Husky, Ned. My wife and I adopted Ned when he was eight years old. He spent the next eight years at our feet and by our side. He was the happiest of dogs. He loved people and cheeseburgers. Our gentle giant. Our Ned Bear.

I began writing this story when he was still alive. It was a creative writing exercise on what I thought he'd be like as an actual bear. When he passed, I found editing this book was a wonderful way to keep his spirit alive. I am thankful for all the amazing memories he gave us and for the inspiration to write this story. Most importantly, I'm thankful for him being such a good dog.

I would like to thank the people who helped me make this book a reality. Without them this story would have been a complete mess.

Laura Perkins was the first person to read this story. She guided me to improve as a storyteller and a writer. Thank you, Laura, for taking the time to answer all my questions as I navigated the seas of becoming an author and learning the ins and outs of publishing.

I am tremendously grateful to my friend, Devin Brooke, who took the time to provide the feedback I needed to improve Ned's tale. You motivated me to push forward when my enthusiasm was beginning to waver. I look forward to discussing the next project with you over salsa and beer.

And a major thank you to Miranda Miller of Editing Realm.

Mostly for not throwing anything at me as I made the same mistakes over and over. Thank you for encouraging me to cut the scenes that only I found interesting and for improving the entire novel. I'm grateful for your patience and your hard work in bringing this story alive.

And finally I'd like to thank all my friends and family for their encouragement over the years to pursue this dream of writing a novel. A special thank you to my parents who have always asked me about my writing and cared. Look mom, I did it!

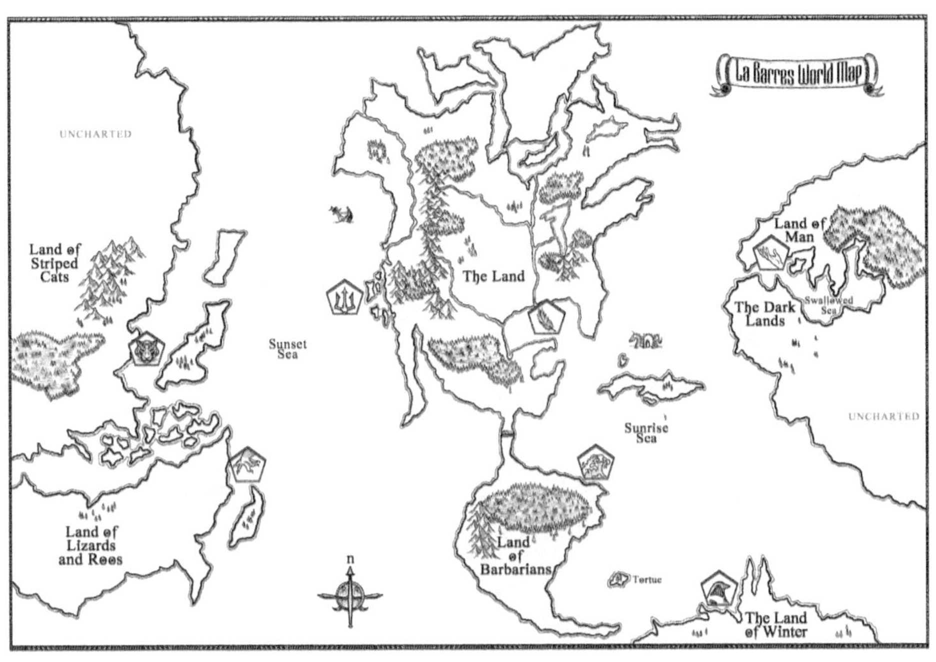
La Barres World Map
UNCHARTED
Land of
Striped
Cats
Land of
Lizards
and Rees
Sunset
Sea
The Land
Land
of
Barbarians
Sunrise
Sea
Tertuc
Land of
Man
The Dark
Lands
Swallowed
Sea
UNCHARTED
The Land
of Winter
n

# About the Author

A.B. Roveen, a former social studies teacher, is a history nerd with a degree from CSUCI. He was born and raised on the coast of southern California where he spent the majority of his adult life. In 2020 he traded in burritos for BBQ, and moved with his family to Missouri. He currently lives there with his wife, their three kids and three dogs. He's an avid baseball and soccer fan and hopes someday he'll see the Angels win another World Series. Like other SoCal natives, he grew up with a fascination for film. He wrote and directed three short films before turning his passion for storytelling and world building into his debut novel.

instagram.com/a.b.roveen

tiktok.com/@a.b.roveen